A WILL TO LIVE

Three True Stories

by Michael Bentinck

MICHAEL BENTINCKS,TITLES ARE
MY DAD MY HERO.ISBN=09526157 11.
FORGOTTEN HEROES.   0952 6157 2X.
A WILL TO LIVE.   0952 6157 03.
WAR TIME WOMEN.   0952 6157 54.
WAVING GOODBYE.   0952 6157 62.
WAR TIME MEMORIES.   0952 6157 46.
www.michaelbentinck.com

CONTENTS

Published by Michael Bentinck © 1996

Typeset in 10½pt New Baskerville
and printed on environmentally-friendly paper
by Print-Out, Histon, Cambridge, UK

ISBN 0 9526157 03

THE BURMA-SIAM RAILWAY

The notorious Burma-Siam railway, built by British, Australian, Dutch and American prisoners of war, was a Japanese project inspired by the need for improved communications to maintain the large Japanese army in Burma. During its construction more than 16,000 prisoners of war died – mainly of sickness, malnutrition and exhaustion – and were buried along the railway. Imprest Burmese and Malay labourers too died in their thousands – exactly how many will never be known. The Japanese kept no records and it was impossible for anyone else to do so, nor were the graves marked, but between 80,000 and 100,000 perished. The railway has been purchased by the Thai Government from its starting point at Ban Pong to the Burmese border, and it is now part of the Royal State railways. It is open to general traffic from Ban Pong to Kanchanaburi, about 33 miles.

Japanese communications depended upon a long and exposed sea route to Rangoon via Singapore and the Strait of Malacca, and a road (quite unfit for prolonged heavy traffic) from Raheng through Kowkareik to Moulmein. The decision to complete the railway connecting Moulmein with Bangkok, which had been commenced before the war but abandoned by the two countries concerned, was taken in June 1942. More than 250 miles of railway, from Thanbyuzayat in Burma to Ban Pong (or Bampong) in Thailand, remained to be constructed, much of it through mountainous country and dense jungle, in a region with one of the worst climates in the world.

The Japanese aimed at completing the railway in 14 months, or at least by the end of 1943. They utilised a labour force composed of prisoners of war taken in the campaigns in South-East Asia and the Pacific, and coolies brought from Malaya and the Dutch East Indies or conscripted in Siam and Burma. From June 1942 onwards large groups of prisoners were transferred periodically to Thailand and Burma from Java, Sumatra and Borneo. Two forces, one based in Thailand and one in Burma, worked from opposite ends of the line towards the centre.

When the first of the prisoners arrived their initial task was the construction of camps at Kanchanaburi and Ban Pong in Thailand, and Thanbyuzayat in Burma. Accommodation for the Japanese guards had to be built first, and at all the staging camps built subsequently along the railway this rule applied. The cook-house and huts for the working parties came next and accommodation for the sick last of all. Frequently men were sent to work on the line long before their accommodation was completed.

Throughout the building of the railway, food supplies were irregular and totally inadequate. Brought up by barge on the Kwai Noi river, or by lorry on a road which was merely a converted jungle track, a consistent service could not be maintained by either method, and rations were nearly always below even the Japanese official scales. Vegetables and other perishables long in transit arrived rotten. The rice was of poor quality, frequently maggoty or in other ways contaminated, and fish, meat, oil, salt and sugar were on a minimum scale. Although it was often possible to supplement this diet by purchases from the local civilian population, men sometimes had to live for weeks on little more than a small daily ration of rice flavoured with salt. Red Cross parcels helped, but these were invariably held up by the Japanese. Malaria, dysentery and pellagra (a vitamin deficiency disease) attacked the prisoners, and the number of sick in the camps was always high.

The Japanese demanded from each camp a certain percentage of its strength for working parties, irrespective of the number of sick, and to make up the required quota the Japanese camp commandants insisted on men totally unfit for work being driven out and sometimes carried out. Those who stayed behind were accommodated in camp 'hospitals' which were simply one or more crude jungle huts. At main camps such as Chungkai, Tamarkan, Non Pladuk and Thanbyuzayat were 'base Hospitals' which were also huts of bamboo and thatch, staffed by such medical officers and orderlies as were allowed by the Japanese to care for the sick prisoners. To these base hospitals desperately sick men – the weak supported by the less weak, since no fit men were allowed to accompany them – were evacuated from the camp hospitals, travelling by the haphazard means of hitch-hiking on a passing lorry or river barge. At both camp and base hospitals, for the greater part of the time, the doctors had only such drugs and equipment as they had been able to carry with them. Neither drugs or surgical instruments were supplied by the Japanese, and although later on certain medical supplies were made available they were always inadequate. A great deal of equipment was improvised by the medical officers and orderlies, and food and medicines were clandestinely obtained. Only the devotion, skill and enterprise of the prisoner of war medical staffs saved the lives of thousands and gradually evolved an organisation which could control disease and mortality.

Work on the railway started at Thanbyuzayat on 1st October 1942 and somewhat later at Ban Pong. The two parties met at Nieke in November 1943, and the line – 263 miles long – was completed by December. Thereafter work on the railway consisted of maintenance, and repairs to damage caused by Allied bombing. Repeated reconnaissance flights over the Burma end of the railway started early in 1943, followed by bombings at intervals. These became more and more frequent when, towards the end of October 1943, trains full of Japanese troops and supplies began to go through from Thailand to Burma. The Japanese would not allow the prisoners to construct a symbol (a white triangle on a blue base) indicating the presence of a prisoner of war camp, and these raids added their quota to the deaths on the line. Most of the camps were right alongside the railway track and some were near bridges and other vulnerable points. The only cover for the prisoners was that afforded by the flimsy bamboo and thatch huts, where they were made to shelter while the raids were in progress, and the inevitable casualties were heavy. In one raid alone on the Non Pladuk area, where the camp was located amongst sidings holding petrol, ammunition and store trains protected by an anti-aircraft post, and prisoners were not allowed to leave the huts, 95 were killed and 300 wounded.

In March 1944, when the bulk of the prisoners were in the main camps at Chungkai, Tamarkan, Kanchanaburi, Tamuan, Non Pladuk and Nakom Paton, conditions temporarily improved. The Japanese had been surprised by the reaction of world opinion against their treatment of prisoners of war, and there is evidence that they began to feel apprehensive about the heavy casualties of 1943, and made efforts to counteract their reputation for uncivilised treatment of prisoners. But this phase soon passed, and from May 1944 until the capitulation of Japan in August 1945 parties of prisoners were sent from the various base camps to work on railway maintenance, cut fuel for the locomotives, and handle stores at dumps along the line. Other parties were employed on cutting and building roads, some through virgin jungle, or in building defence positions.

The graves of those who died during the construction and maintenance of the Burma-Siam railway (except Americans, who were repatriated) have been transferred from the camp burial grounds and solitary sites along the railway into three war cemeteries. At Chungkai War Cemetery and Kanchanaburi War Cemetery in Thailand now rest those recovered from the southern part of the line, from Ban Pong to Nieke, about half its length. In the War Cemetery at Thanbyuzayat in Burma lie those from the northern half of the line.

Those who have no known grave are commemorated by name on memorials elsewhere; the land forces on either the Rangoon Memorial or the Singapore Memorial and the naval casualties on memorials at the manning ports.

INTRODUCTION

The book you are about to read is made up of three true stories given to me by three remarkable men. The first story of Jim Bentinck, my own dear father, is another story of his time spent with the Japanese Executioner that he shared with me in the last three months of his life. Many of you will have read "My Dad My Hero" (ISBN No. 09526157 1 1) and "Forgotten Heroes" (ISBN No. 09526157 2 X) and will know much about his time with the little man of death.

In the seven months my father had as the Executioner's driver, he had the job of burying thousands of those put to death. He told me how he felt sure that they were all innocent people who were just caught up in a living nightmare. In those seven months he managed to steal six photos from the front of the truck that he drove the Executioner in. The Executioner would always take a photo of his killings and when he collected his photos he would lay them in the front of the truck. When he stopped to do his killings my father was made to sit in the truck until he had finished, it was then that my father would take a chance and steal one of these photos and hide it in his shorts, for he knew it would prove to others the things he was being witness to every day. My father hid these photos in a hollowed out piece of bamboo and managed to get them through his three and a half years of captivity.

As he shared his stories of those times with me in the last few months of his life, it was only after he had told me everything and just a couple of days before he died that he told me about these photos and where I could find them. All I knew was that they were photos, he never said what they were of, only to say that it would prove to me that all he had told me was true. He asked me not to get them until he was dead, which I did, and when I saw these horrific photos I knew all that he had told me was true.

Our second story is of another very brave man and now a very dear friend to my wife and I. It is the true story of Stanley Chown MBE who was one of the lucky ones to survive the death camp at Sonkari. Stanley was a first class chef and you will see how he saved many of his comrades' lives by cooking dishes that you and I would not dream of eating. It shows us the courage and bravery that was needed to survive against the odds and certainly of how your love for your fellow man can get you through such horrific times. I know how privileged I am to be the first to hear Stanley's story and I am pleased to share it with you all now.

Our third story is of another hero, Mr Percy Legge. He not only survived the death railway but also survived his trip to Japan and the nightmare of working down a coal mine in such unsafe conditions. He really is one of the lucky ones to have come through it all. I shall never forget the emotions we shared together as I took down his story for, as you will see, it is such a moving story – as they all are. I would like to think all three stories have a mixture of love and goodness overcoming evil and as Percy and all my FEPOW friends have stressed on me, it was sheer comradeship and true togetherness that got them all through as they walked through that valley of death.

DEDICATION

This book is dedicated to all who suffered at the hands of the Japanese in world war two. History now shows us that hundreds of thousands of people died horrific deaths; people of all nationalities, people like the dear nurses of Alexandra Hospital at Singapore, the poor women taken as comfort women who were used in such a degrading way that those of them left alive today still feel so unclean.

To all the brave men that suffered so much as prisoners of the Japanese, those who suffered on the death railway and for those who worked in the mines and factories of Japan as prisoners.

To the memory of all those that gave the ultimate sacrifice and laid down their lives for King and Country, for to them we owe our today, a thing we must never forget.

At the time of writing this book, much is being said of whether we should keep observing the two minutes silence on Remembrance Day. My own feelings are that it is something mankind should observe until the end of time, for the men of every nation that laid down their lives for their fellow man in times of war, for none of us today can ever repay them for our freedom.

Our FEPOW prayer of Remembrance says "as we that are left grow old with the years, remembering the heartache and pain and tears, hoping and praying that never again man will sink to such sorrow and shame, the price that was paid we will always remember every day, every month, not just in November". Loving my own father as I did and still do, although he has gone to that far better place, it is a thing I think about and remember every day of what he had to do and see as a young man of 20 years old. He had to see such horrific things – things that no one should ever have to see at any age, let alone at the tender age of 20. So to all those mentioned above and to my dear father, I dedicate this book to them and thank them all for my life today.

For the Fallen

They shall grow not old, as we that are left grow old, age shall not weary them, nor the years condemn, at the going down of the sun and in the morning we will remember them.

Lest We Forget

You my friends must be the judges of the stories but I assure you they are all true and that is why the last chapter of the book is a letters section, letters from you, my readers; letters that show of how to this day that nightmare time still haunts so many of you. I hope you will find the book of interest, and in a way I'm sure that you will know what I mean when I say enjoy reading it.

Once again I thank you for your support in helping me to be able to help the Far Eastern Prisoners of War Association to help care for those still suffering these 52 years on.

✧　✧　✧　✧　✧

FOREWORD

By John Ezard of The Guardian

Mike Bentinck has done me the honour of asking me to write a foreword to this, his third book. Last year I had the privilege of reading before publication his second book, Forgotten Heroes, with its magnificent story of how his late father managed to retain a gentle, deeply decent human heart during his almost unthinkable experiences as a kind of slave-assistant to the Japanese chief executioner in occupied Singapore.

That book told us how Jim Bentinck sang a verse of the Cambridgeshires' hymn, 'Abide With Me' over each of the many thousand beheaded, mostly Asian men, women and children he was forced to bury in a mass grave; how he also spoke over them a verse from book 21, verse four of Revelations. The verse is moving to quote because it is so beautiful – and reading it so conscientiously was such a beautiful act in those circumstances – that it almost has the effect of carrying out the divine promise made in the words. It comes close to taking away the horror, the pain, the grief and the deaths:

And God shall wipe away all tears from their eyes; and there shall be no more death, neither sorrow nor crying; neither shall there be any more pain; for the former things are passed away.

Choosing and reciting that was all this heartbroken, sick, underfed, defenceless, frightened, leaderless teenage British soldier had the power to do at the time; and he did it, by natural decent instinct, in exactly the right way. Out of everything I have read and heard of, his is one of the quietly noblest gestures in the history of warfare. It does the human race credit, it pulls us back from the abyss and the torture-pit. The Cambridge Evening News, which is part of the trade in which I work, probably never knew what a remarkable fellow it had in its employment. A Will To Live discloses that he did think he had saved a young Thai boy. It was just one brand plucked from the burning; but I'm sure I won't be alone in letting out a cheer on reading that passage. Would you or I have risked as much?

Nothing, though, can quite take away the pain in the heart, which is more acute even than pain in the body. Jim Bentinck's later life was a testament to that fact. It is true, though in some cases mercifully less so, of the others whose story his son has come to tell. Of Mike Bentinck, one of the veterans says in the new book you are about to read, "We feel as if you are one of us now". He has not only retold these plain stories of old, unsung griefs but taken them into his heart as fully as someone born in a later generation can. If the rest of my generation and Mike's had done this as fully as he has, our own children and grandchildren would be growing up in greater certainty of no more wars.

ACKNOWLEDGEMENTS

My thanks go to the three men whose true stories you will read in this book . To "MY DAD MY HERO" who opened his heart and soul to me, in the last three months of his life, and although I did not realise it then, it was to change my life so very much.

To Stanley Chown, MBE and Percy Legge for sharing their stories with me and for allowing me to share them with you. To their dear wives, Joyce and Dora, for the help they gave to me in preparing the book, and above all for the help and love they have given to their brave husbands through their lives together. To all my FEPOW friends who send me photos and memorabilia of that nightmare time in their lives, while they were prisoners of the Japanese. To the many friends I have made through doing radio appearances across the country.

To my friends at Print-Out, my publishers, for their hard work and help they have given to me since I wrote my first book. To my own dear wife and family, especially Beverley who typed the original manuscript, for all their help, love and support.

To all the friends I have made while giving talks at Womens' Institutes and village societies, and for the many FEPOW groups that have allowed me to be their after-dinner speaker – as I always say at the time, it really is an honour and a privilege for me to be among my"HEROES".

Mostly I thank you, my readers, for to you I owe so much, for without you my dear readers, I could not begin to help the Far Eastern Prisoners of War who gave and suffered so much for our today.

LOOKING BACK

Courtesy of Cambridge Newspapers Ltd

■ FROM THE *NEWS* OF SEPTEMBER, 1945.

OF THE 7,000 Allied prisoners who were forced by the Japs to work on the construction of the Burma- Siam railway, only 3,100 returned to Singapore. Three thousand, mainly British and Australians, were buried in Siam. Many died on the journey back.

The facts were disclosed today in a report quoted by Singapore radio by Major Wilde, a British prisoner.

■ FROM THE *NEWS* OF SEPTEMBER, 1945.

GENERAL Hideki Tojo, Japanese Prime Minister at the time of the treacherous Pearl Harbour attack in 1941, shot himself today as US officers arrived to arrest him at his home in Yogamachi, on the outskirts of Tokyo.

Captain James Johnson, an American doctor, who is treating him, said later: "Tojo has a good chance of surviving."

Tojo was given a blood transfusion and gasped and groaned while the doctor stitched up the wound.

■ FROM THE *NEWS* OF AUGUST, 1945.

TWO days after VJ-Day, and the official Japanese surrender, General MacArthur was ordering the Japs to "quit stalling". Four American bombers, on a photographic mission over the Tokyo Bay area to- day, were attacked by ten Japanese fighters and moderate to intense anti-aircraft fire, says a report from Okinawa. One bomber was badly shot up, but none of the crew was hurt.

■ FROM THE *NEWS* OF NOVEMBER, 1945.

MR Atlee, British Prime Minister, broke away from his atomic energy talks with President Truman today to warn the world in a speech to a joint session of Congress that civilisation must accept the Christian principle before it was too late.

"The United Nations organisation, in which I profoundly believe, must be something more than an agreement between governments. It must be an expression of the will of the common people in every country."

■ FROM THE *NEWS* OF DECEMBER, 1945.

CAMBRIDGE'S Guildhall — its civic centre — was last night an occasion whose memory will live so long as wars are remembered. It was the Town's welcome to her sons — men of the Cambridgeshires, the Suffolks and the Norfolks, Sappers of the Royal Engineers, as well as representatives of the Royal Navy and the RAF — recently repatriated from prisoners of war camps in the Far East.

The Christmas Party was, without doubt, the success the organisers hoped.

■ FROM THE *NEWS* OF JANUARY, 1946.

TWENTY-four people are feared to have died when an RAF Transport Command Dakota, bringing home former British prisoners of war from Singapore, crashed during the night in a blizzard at Callelongue, near Marseilles.

Only three of the plane's 27 occupants survived, authoritative British circles in Paris stated today.

A fourth survivor died while being carried on a stretcher along icy paths from the scene of the crash.

■ FROM THE *NEWS* OF JANUARY, 1946.

THE Cambridgeshire Regiment are in receipt of some astounding news.

The regimental drums, which were lost at Singapore, are reported safe. The news is contained in a letter from Miss C. Mary Taylor, Welfare Officer, S.E.A.C. Red Cross, Singapore, in which she says.

"Quite by chance I have found eight Cambridgeshire Regimental drums and have got permission to ship them home."

■ FROM THE *NEWS* OF OCTOBER, 1946.

INTO the sunny setting of Cambridge's peaceful Market Square, mellow in the light of a perfect early Autumn afternoon, the minds of hundreds of ex-soldiers gathered there yesterday projected never-to-be forgotten memories of a last stand in Singapore, the mud and blood of Flanders and the veldt and kopjes of South Africa.

CHAPTER ONE

Jim Bentinck's True Stories of his Time with the Japanese Executioner

Jim Bentinck was in the 1st Battalion of the Cambridgeshire Regiment in A Company. He was a nineteen year old private in 1942 when Singapore fell to the Japanese. Many of you will have read his true story in the books "My Dad My Hero" and "Forgotten Heroes" and I could not start this book without sharing another true story that he shared with me as he lay dying in Ely RAF Hospital. Many of you will know by now that Jim was my own dear late father and I am just so privileged that when the doctors told him that they thought he only had three months to live because the tropical worms he carried in his blood had damaged his heart so much, although it was a great shock to us all, he decided that at least he would talk to me about those nightmare days he had spent as driver and assistant to the main Japanese Executioner for Singapore.

Jim already knew how lucky he had been to survive the Alexandra Hospital massacre, the day before General Percival signed the surrender. A day that Jim and thousands of others would never forget. Yes, Sunday the 15th February 1942 would live on in the minds of those people for the rest of their lives. For it was the day that hell on earth began for them. I have said many times that the only people to know the real meaning of the word suffering besides those poor Jews in the Nazi death camps are our own Far Eastern Prisoners of War (FEPOWS) and through the course of this book you will see why.

In those last three months I spent with my dear father, I was to find out just what a hero I had as my father. I was to find out why ever since I had been a child he had woken up our household every other night through having his nightmares, yet he would never talk about them. I think he found in those last three months with me that he wished he had spoken to me a lot sooner about the horrific things he had seen and suffered, as not long before he died, as we cuddled together in his little hospital room, he looked up at me and said "son, I am sorry that I have laid all of this on to you but I do feel better for sharing it with you". I gripped him tight to me and told him "you old fool, you should have shared it with me years ago, it might have helped with your nightmares

13

and let us all get a night's sleep". We then laughed at one another, a thing I shall never forget as I shall never forget those stories he shared with me. I often now have nightmares about them but I talk them out with all my FEPOW friends and as they tell me, "Michael," they say, "you have taken so much on yourself and researched this war so much that you might as well have been there with us". They tell me "we feel as if you are one of us now" and I can tell you now that is all the thanks I need in my efforts to help these brave men. For as you know, they are all my heroes.

I share with you now another of the stories my father shared with me of his time with the Japanese Executioner. On the day of surrender, Jim was released from the outhouse at Alexandra Hospital that the Japs had forced him and many others into, even though he had been badly wounded through the groin and was not really fit to stand. As he was let out he was informed by the Jap Officer that they were now prisoners of the Japanese, as General Percival had signed the surrender. He informed them it was a thing the Japanese would never do as it would disgrace their glorious Emperor and now they were to become guests of the Emperor (what a way to treat guests!). They were then told "you must all now march the 21-odd miles to Changi Prison". Jim and the others with him were rounded up in the Hospital grounds at the rear of the Hospital and it was here that Jim saw what the Japs had done to the nurses from the Hospital. It was near to the Hospital's oil storage tanks that Jim saw with his own eyes the nurses being raped by the Jap soldiers. The British Officer with Jim complained angrily to the Jap Officer who had taken charge of the Hospital but he was just knocked to the ground and told "You no say anything. You prisoner. It now up to us if you live or die". It was only after the war that Jim found out that these dear nurses had not just been raped but had been killed as well, one thing I knew he could not forgive the Japanese for.

Jim reached Changi Prison only to find it so overcrowded and it was not long before he was moved to River Valley Camp. Those of you that have read "My Dad My Hero" will know that it was while here he was taken by the Japanese Executioner as his driver and assistant. It was at the threat of life or death to him and, as he told me, at nineteen life is so precious, as all life is, that you just want to stay alive. It was soon after the fall of Singapore and Jim found that the Executioner was one of the head ones of the Japanese Kempei-Tai. He told me that the Nazi SS would have learnt plenty from these nasty little men who took great delight in their work of inflicting torture and death on their captives.

One day in May 1942 Jim drove the Executioner and the two armed guards that he always had with him to Changi Prison to collect an Australian Officer. Jim said "hello" to this Officer and was quickly told "you no speak to him, he no good man." Jim winked to the Australian who smiled and winked back at him. Jim was told to drive to the Ford Motor Universal Motor Works in Orchard Road, the building the Kempei-Tai were using as their headquarters. On arrival the Australian Officer was taken by the two armed guards into the building. The Executioner told Jim to stay with the truck in the yard, the gates were shut and an armed Jap guard stood at the gate. As Jim sat waiting he could hear the screams coming from inside the building, not just screams from one person but from many and Jim felt sure some of the screams were coming from women and children. The Japanese guard walked over to Jim and gave him a cigarette, he smiled at Jim and said "this no good place" Jim knew this only too well. The guard was only about the same age as Jim and told Jim that his father had been to America and had learnt him some English. He asked Jim if he was to come here often would he help him learn more English. Jim wondered about this for a moment then said "I teach you English, you teach me Japanese" and over the next few months this is what they did. Jim found this to be a life saver in his time on the death railway as all numbering etc. had to be done in Japanese.

After what seemed like hours the Australian Officer was bought out and dumped in the truck, Jim could see he had been beaten . The Executioner looked across at Jim as he sat in beside him and said "back to Changi". Jim was to pick this poor Officer up for the next six days and take him to the Kempei-Tai headquarters. Every day Jim could see that the Officer could not go on for much longer and on the sixth day the Officer never came out with the Executioner and guards but a few days later while Jim sat waiting for some other poor soul, he had chance to speak to the Jap guard that he had been helping with English and he told Jim that he thought the Australian Officer had been killed as he saw the truck that took the bodies away and felt sure he had seen the Officers body put on this truck. Jim never did find out what this young Officer had done but he often heard the Executioner say the name Gordon Bennett to him and Jim knew this was the Australian Commanding Officer that had got away before the surrender. Jim wondered if the Japs thought this young Officer had anything to tell them about how Bennett had got away. Whatever it was they wanted to know the young Officer had paid with his life.

In the seven months Jim had with the Executioner he spent many hours waiting at Orchard Road and the screams he heard and the things

15

he saw were to stay with him for the rest of his life. He told me he felt the only good thing about the place was the young Jap guard who had shown him kindness and he told me if it had not have been a time of war, he felt he could have made friends with the young guard. He told me how there were a few Japanese who could be kind to you but if the other Japs saw this they soon saw to it that their own suffered as much as you.

One day soon after the death of the young Australian Officer, Jim was sitting waiting at Orchard Road for the Executioner when three large lorries drew into the yard. The Japanese drivers got out and walked over to where Jim was sitting in his truck and started to prod Jim with their pickle sticks. They were ranting on at him and Jim could not make out what they were saying. After what seemed like ages to Jim of being hit and prodded about by these Jap drivers, the young Japanese guard who Jim was helping with his English appeared. He shouted out at the Jap drivers and at once they stopped hitting out at Jim. They then walked back to their lorries and started to roll up the canvas roofing that covered the tops of the back of the lorries. Jim asked the young Jap guard why they had picked on him and was told "because they see you prisoner, they want you to do their work for them, and roll back the covers on trucks but as soon as I tell them you Executioners driver they know they must stop". He then said to Jim "I no talk any more to you now. It not be good with these others here". Jim quite understood this and was only too pleased to be left to sit on his own and be left alone. Jim did notice that when the backs of the lorries were uncovered that on the front of each one there was a machine gun. After hours of waiting the Executioner and the two guards came out with a Chinese man. Jim could see that this man was in a bad way, he had been badly beaten and all his finger nails had been pulled out. Jim was ordered to drive down to the docks. As Jim drove along he could hear the poor Chinese man lay groaning on the floor of the truck. Jim knew by now that this poor man was to be killed for he had driven many others to meet their death here. Once down at the docks the Japanese guards rounded up all the Chinese who were working there, and also some of the allied prisoners that were in work parties at the docks. They were all rounded up and lined up to watch this poor man meet his maker. The two guards made the man kneel down and Jim felt sure as he knelt down he knew what was to be his fate, it seemed as if he knew his suffering would soon be over.

The Executioner shouted out something to all those that had been forced to watch and then with a swish of his large samurai sword it was all over. The poor mans head lay severed from his body and for him it

16

was all over. Jim knew what was expected of him now but he always waited until the Executioner said to him "you put head on pole and put body in back of truck". As Jim was carrying out this gruesome task the three lorries that he had seen at Orchard Road, the Kempei-Tai headquarters, arrived. Two of them were crammed full of Chinese of all ages, and into the empty lorry the Japs forced all the other Chinese that they had lined up to watch the Executioner. Jim could see that many of these people were only young teenagers of both sexes. Some of them panicked and started to run away. Jim watched in horror as they were just shot in the back as they ran, then one of the Jap guards would just walk up to where they lay and run his bayonet through their heart. Jim was sick of the sight of this by now but as many of you know, it was a thing he lived with in his mind for the next 45 years.

Once the panic calmed down, Jim was ordered to load the dead bodies onto the back of his truck with the man that had been beheaded. As he did this, he was wondering to himself what would be the fate of all these people, whom he believed numbered about 200. He was soon to find out as the Executioner shouted at him "you be quick now, we go". Jim got into the drivers seat beside the man of death and was told to drive off to the beach, which he did, the three lorries following on behind. As Jim drove along he sat with thoughts rushing through his head of what was to be the fate of these poor helpless people, but in his heart he already knew, for he had already seen in the three weeks before the fall of Singapore how thousands of them had tried to get on to a ship to flee from what they must have known in their hearts would happen if the Japanese won the day, for they knew what the Japanese had been doing to their own country folk in China for nearly 10 years. They knew they would receive no mercy from the Japanese, for those who could not board a ship and get away, there was nowhere, and they had to seek refuge wherever they could find it.

As Jim drove along he was thinking of those last few days of fighting and of how lucky he had been to escape death but he knew there was to be no escape for these poor people. As he approached every road junction, which were all manned by Japanese sentries, he and the three lorries were just waved right through. Jim thought to himself it was all to plan for the Japanese, as if the sentries knew they were coming, for Jim knew that any other time they would have to stop as he had done many times before, even with the Executioner with him. He would be made to stop and papers would be checked, for this was how it was now for everyone. Jim had picked up the bodies of many of these people since the Japanese took over, people who did not have their identification papers in order were often beaten to death on the spot as the Jap sentries vented their anger on them. Jim would often have to pick their bodies up with the Executioner and many times they would be beheaded even though already dead then Jim and the Executioner would take their heads to public places like Dhoby Ghaut and Kallang Bridge and place the heads on show as a deterrent to others. Jim told me that with such deterrents crime was negligible, for even the most petty crime was dealt with very severely by the Japanese. He told me "it was like going back hundreds of years when if you were caught stealing, you lost your hand etc. for this is what was happening now". They were now coming to the beach and Jim could see that the whole area was crammed full with Japs. Jim was ordered to pull over to the side of the road and allow the lorries to pass by him, which he did.

He could now see the faces of the Chinese people as they came past. He told me how they seemed quite calm, as if they knew there was no escape for them and as if they seemed in a trance-like state, yet he told me he could never forget their faces. The lorries drove straight down on to the beach and side by side they reversed back to the sea. The Jap soldiers already on the beach let the tail boards of the lorries down and at this time Jim was sitting in the truck with the Executioner beside him. They were in the centre of the beach and had a good view of right along the coast. He could see that about 30 Japanese armed soldiers were lined up in front of their lorries and as the Chinese were bundled out of them, Jim heard the soldiers' rifle bolts click back ready, then the three lorries pulled forward to just in front of the Jap soldiers. The drivers and the armed guards that had been sitting beside them both jumped on to the rear of the lorry and manned the machine gun. By now some of the Chinese were starting to panic and many of them had started to run; these the armed soldiers picked off. Jim told me he felt sure while this was going on that one or two of the younger men fell to the sea in the hope of swimming away if they could. The Executioner stood up in the truck beside Jim and raised his arm. When he lowered it all hell let loose. The machine guns opened up and there were screams and bodies fell. Jim told me "they had no chance, it was sheer murder – just one great massacre". It was soon over and then the Jap soldiers moved in with their bayonets to finish off anyone left alive. Then he saw a Japanese gun boat come along and he could see they were machine gunning into the water so he knew that those who had tried to find freedom by feigning death and swimming away had not found it. He told me he felt sick to the stomach. He was now just turned 21 years old and wondered what he had done to be involved in such a nightmare – a nightmare that was to live with him for the rest of his life; for how could anyone take away the sights he was having to see. One thing he did see when all the killing was over was that six very good looking young Chinese girls had been spared and were being held by Japanese soldiers at the edge of the beach. They were already naked and Jim could see that the soldiers were throwing the girls clothes to one another. At this time the Executioner said to Jim "we go now" and so Jim drove off knowing in his mind what was to be the fate of these young girls, for as he told me "they were now the spoils of war and objects of fun for these soldiers". He told me "imagine what they must have gone through at the hands of those 30 or more Jap soldiers before they met their death".

As I sat and imagined the fate of these poor girls, I knew all too well what had happened to them and I said to my father "how can people forgive such things?' He looked at me and said "you cannot son, only God can forgive them". He looked at me and with tears running down his face he said "Michael, when the Romans crucified our Lord, in his last breath, as a spear was thrust into his side, he said 'FORGIVE THEM FATHER FOR THEY KNOW NOT WHAT THEY DO'. In the last few days I have left Michael, I wish I could say that. But hand on heart I cannot do that Michael, for what they did was just murder, there is no other word for it. For what they did there is no excuse. One human should never do that to another human". He told me how he had faced death himself many times at the hands of his captors during his time on the death railway as many of you will have read in "My Dad My Hero" and of how he could never forget the times he had watched his mates beaten to death in front of him knowing that if he or any of the others tried to help their comrade, they would just be killed on the spot. He told me how he had seen some men choose death like this instead of the day to day suffering, as at least then their suffering was over. It was those left alive that were suffering in their struggle to stay alive. Then as I cuddled him to me he told me how he had lost his best friend like this – a friend he had grown up with in Newnham, Cambridgeshire... Kenny Baines, a Private in the 1st Battalion of the Cambridgeshire's No. 5933426. He told me how the record books showed that Kenny died in Burma while a prisoner on the death railway but what it should say is that Kenny was already dying from tropical illness but was forced out of the sick hut and picked on by the guards until he fell dead. He told me "that's murder, Michael, no other word for it. I have seen Kenny in my dreams many times now Michael, not always as lads playing in Grantchester Meadows but mainly he comes to me in that death railway camp as he is being beaten to death and he is begging me for help, a help that I could not give him. Michael I know now that I shall soon see my dear friend Kenny again and perhaps he will forgive me for not helping him and dying with him that day". By now we were both in floods of tears and as I cuddled him to me, I told him "Kenny will know what it was like for you dad, he will know that if any of you had stepped forward to help him, it would have been the end for you too and I think he will know there is nothing to forgive you for". I often now think of that far better place we can go to after our time on this earth and I think of my dad and Kenny and all those dear FEPOWS at our Lord's right hand side for I for one feel sure our Lord has a special place for all these brave souls in paradise.

Since writing these books I have heard from many people who knew my dad and Kenny as young lads and many have written to me to say how in the last few weeks of leave before they set sail for the Far East, that Kenny and my dad visited them to say goodbye. Many of them have told me that when my dad said "I don't know when I shall ever see you again" Kenny would say 'I shall not see you again, as I won't get through this war' to which they would reply 'don't talk daft Kenny, you will soon be back with us' but of course, we know now that Kenny was right. But does this mean he went off to war unprepared in his mind or was it all meant to be – part of that big unknown plan that none of us can ever know, for as you know, none of us know the time or the place when we shall be called, the only thing we can be sure of is that it will come. For Jim he knew he would come home, for he would believe nothing else, he told everyone "my dad came through the first world war and came home and I am going to do the same". Positive thinking I hear you say, and yes I am sure it was, and who knows it could have been that that brought him home, for you will know by now from reading my other books just how many times he had looked death in the face and had lived to tell the tale. I then said "Dad, what happened after you left that horrific scene on the beach?". "We drove back to Orchard Road to their headquarters and after dropping off the Executioner, I and the two armed guards drove to the mass grave on the outskirts of Singapore, where we put the bodies we had in the back of the truck. The two Jap guards would stand and have a smoke and watch me as I lowered the victims into their final resting place. They never stopped me from reading the passage from my army prayer book over them". As many of you will know it was Revelations Chapter Two: "and God shall wipe away all tears from their eyes and there shall be no more death, neither sorrow nor crying, neither shall there be any more pain". After Jim had read this passage over them, he would sing a verse from his favourite hymn

'Abide with me' – the Cambridgeshire's hymn. I knew then as I was losing my dear father that this would be one of the hymns and certainly the reading that I would read over him at his funeral and this is what I did. A day I shall never forget, October 6th 1990.

But now I said "Dad, was that it for that day for you?" Back came his reply, "oh no, I then took the two guards back to Orchard Road and would sit and wait for the Executioner. The screams coming from that building always sounded much worse at night and as I sat there a shiver would run right through my body and I would wonder if it would one day be my turn to suffer in that torture chamber. I knew this could happen at any time if the Executioner took an instant dislike to me but I always thought to myself that he would just execute me by taking my head off as this seemed to be his favourite way of killing people. It was a thing I thought about many times as I sat waiting for him as I have told you before son. Many times I thought that death would be better than the things I was having to see and do each day but I was young and life meant so much to me and all I could think of was the thought of coming home again to make a better life for myself and your mum and to see my dear mum and dad again and my kid sister. I knew they were praying for me Michael, and I like to think that those prayers were heard and helped me through those four years of hell and anyway, if I had not come home I would have not had you son, so you see it was a good job I never gave in at those times that I was near to death. I must have been meant to come home for there was always someone watching over me to help me through. I must tell you though son, when I got that snipers bullet through my groin, I thought my chance of ever being a father had gone, for he damn near took my wedding tackle clean off and I know it was only thanks to the skill of the surgeon at Alexandra Hospital that you are here today with me son". We then made a private joke about it and shared a good laugh together, which was good after the weeks of crying that we had done together. I then said "come on dad, tell me what happened when the Executioner came out". "Well it was usually about 9.30pm when he came out and he would say to me 'you take me big house, Adams Road'. This was now a comfort house for the Japanese Officers and Kempei-Tai where you can imagine what went on. I would be left to sit outside waiting with the two armed guards, who would gesture to me as to what the Executioner would be doing. As we sat there, sometimes the guards would give me a cigarette, and although they could not speak English, we managed to make one another understand what we meant. They would show me pictures of their wives and family back home and say "this place no good, better Japan" to which I would think to myself 'England even better!'. There would be other drivers waiting for Jap Officers and sometimes I would be allowed to chat with them while the Jap guards chatted to the other guards. I often met a chap called Jack Clark who I think was in the Beds and Herts Regiment. He drove a little Jap Officer who was only about 4' 6" tall and was very fat. We used to sit and say to one another, pity the poor girl that has to look after him, but he was very good to Jack for he had been educated in England and could speak perfect English and told Jack that while he was a young man in England that English people were very good and kind to him, so he was good to Jack and while he was in the comfort house he would leave Jack some food to eat and Jack always shared this with me, and if I had any extra food I would share it with him. It was like an evening picnic, and Jack and I would exchange stories of what we had seen happen through the course of the day which when we got back to camp we would pass on to others – all part of the grapevine news. At about 11.30pm out would come the little Executioner. You could tell he had been drinking but it did not make him bad tempered, just the opposite. He would say 'Jim you good man. You do as I say, you be OK'. Sometimes when he was drunk he would give me some money, not much, but it all helped. Once back at his Officers quarters, I would drop him off, then I and the two guards would put the truck up for the night and they would see that I was taken in to my hut".

"Billy or one of my mates would have saved my rice ration for me and I would wake them and share with them any food I had managed to get for them, then we would sit for a while and talk about everything we had been through that day. They would tell me of the work parties that they had been in and of how some poor chap had been beaten up and was now dying in the sick hut. I would give them the money I had and ask them if they could get away from their work party tomorrow and try to buy something helpful for the lads in the sick hut, for I had taken my share of kindness from others on the many occasions that I had laid ill in the sick hut and knew only too well how it had been this extra food that had got me through and not the six ounces of rice slop the Japs allowed you each day. There was no medication given by the Japs for our lads so anything we could get from the locals like this was a life saver for someone".

"As we sat and talked of what we had been doing that day, we always thought of our loved ones at home and wondered what they were doing or if they were all right, for we did not know for sure whether Hitler had invaded our dear old England and we would fall asleep most nights talking like this. Morning soon came and I would find the two guards at my hut ready for another day – sometimes it would be at the crack of dawn and they would walk me to the truck. I would check the oil and water etc. and check the engine. I never did have any engine oil for it, just old cooking oil from the Japanese cook house but that old truck never broke down in the seven months I drove it. Once the truck was checked and ready, we went to collect the Executioner, then he would be driven to the Kempei-Tai headquarters and after waiting anything up to two or three hours for him, he would emerge and jump in the truck beside me and tell me where to drive him to Sometimes it would be to just pick up some poor Chinese or Malays to bring back for questioning, but most times it was a one way trip for these poor people; they never came out of these torture places alive. If I did not take them to Orchard Road it was to the YMCA building in Stamford Road which was their east headquarters. I also took him to a big house in Smith Street which was their west district branch, also the central police station in South Bridge Road. These were their main headquarters for their Kempei-Tai interrogations but really Michael, they were just torture chambers and houses of death. I can still hear the screams coming from them now in my head, a noise I shall never be able to forget. Some days we would just take over timber yards and if the locals working there put up any resistance, they were killed on the spot. I was left to sit in the truck and watch these massacres and I often thought that one day they would kill me too, knowing as they did that I was witness to all they had done and were doing. Thankfully for me that did not happen but I always thought it would. In all the times these raids were going on I was only ever able to help one man escape death; yes, he was just one out of thousands that were killed. I told you about how on one raid at a timber yard the Executioner cut off the mans hands, as he waived them about in the air screaming "you no take my yard and my wood" well it was only a few days after this that we raided another timber yard. I say 'we' as I was with them, if only as the Executioner's driver. I am still with them, to this day. I wish it could have been someone else instead of me Michael but alas it was not to be. Anyway, it was late in the afternoon when this particular timber yard was raided and I already had about twenty odd dead bodies on the back of the truck. On these occasions there was always two other trucks with us to take the wood away, and about six armed soldiers. There would be no questions asked – just drive in, then these Jap soldiers would open up and kill everyone in sight. On this occasion, while all the shooting and shouting was going on, I was left as usual sitting in the truck while the Executioner and the two armed guards stood watching the killing going on. As I sat there I felt someone get on

23

the back of the truck, as I looked round this young Thai lad was looking straight at me, he just smiled at me and fell on top of the other dead bodies. I just sat quiet and kept my eyes looking forward in the hope that he had not been seen. After the massacre, I was ordered to load the dead bodies on to the truck while the soldiers and the Executioner's two guards loaded the wood and machinery onto the other two lorries. I put about another seven bodies on the back of my truck and loaded them all on top of the young lad. It must have really been his lucky day for when all was finished at this yard, darkness was falling and the Executioner wanted to get going so he left the two armed guards with the other soldiers and instructed me to drive him back to camp, which I did. I dropped him off at his quarters and he told me to go and bury the dead, which I did. To do this I had to go past more guards and felt sure they would check the dead by bayoneting them in the heart as they often did, but to my amazement they just looked at me and waved me through. I drove up to the grave pit which was only some twenty yards away from these guards. As I got out of the truck my heart was pumping so fast my hands were sweating and yes I was shaking with fear, the headlights of the truck was the only light I had now to see the grave by. I started to lift the bodies out and place them in the grave. I soon came to the young lad and he looked up at me, he never said a word, we just looked at one another. I knew only too well what would happen to me if we were found out. I lifted him out and he lay in my arms as if he were dead. I laid him on the top of the other bodies in the grave and as I did I looked towards the camp fence as much to say there's the way out old son if you can get through the wire. He knew what I was trying to gesture to him and nothing needed to be said. I laid the other bodies in the grave and scattered some earth over them, then I stood and read my reading and sang a verse over them, knowing that the Jap guards would expect me to as I always did this. Once I had done this I got back into the truck and drove to where I always left it, then I made my way to my hut, my heart still banging away in my chest as if it was going to explode any second. As I went into the hut a couple of the blokes were still up sitting talking. They said 'you alright tonight Jim? We've saved some rice for you, have you been able to get anything extra for us Jim?' I replied 'yes, a young Thai lad'. 'What?' they said, 'where is he?'. I then told them the full story to which one of them replied 'you must be mad Jim, you know what would have happened to you if you had been caught'. The other blokes smiled and said 'good for you Jim, well done mate'. As I sat and ate my rice I felt good for once. I knew I had done something good at last when there was nothing but death around me every day. It felt so good to me that I had been able to help save just one life. I slept like a log that night, which is a strange thing really but I did, and when we awoke at sunrise, I went off to check at the grave as I knew how I had left the soil over him and yes he had gone. I don't know if he survived the war Michael, but I hope he did. I have often thought of him and I would like to think after escaping death like that, that he went on to have a good and full life. I would also like to think that the young Jap soldier that I used to speak to at Orchard Road went on to have a life as well. I never saw him again after that but not long before I was sent off to work on the death railway I did hear that he had been sent off to fight at the Burma front. I will never forget his kindness to me; he would slip me some fruit or a few cigarettes at very great risk to himself, so Michael don't think all Japanese are bad. It takes all sorts old son to make this funny old world of ours".

"Don't blame them for what they did to me son, they were a complete different culture to us and their Emperor and his Regime had them all brainwashed. He had them believing he was their God and you know there is only one true God and he is a God of love son, for he led me through the paths of hell and brought me out to have a life but why all my young mates had to die such terrible deaths I can't make out yet. But when I meet my maker it will be one of the things I shall be asking him son". I looked at my dad and said to him "you are a one-off, do you know that? One minute you tell me you cannot forgive them for what they did as it was just murder, now you tell me not to blame them for the pain they put you through. How can I ever forgive them dad for hurting someone I love so much?" "Michael," he said, "I have carried enough hatred in my heart for the both of us, perhaps that's why it is giving out on me now. What you can do for me now son is to try and make our world a better place for us all to live in. Everything is there for us son, if only mankind could learn to share, there need be no more wars or suffering; we could all live as God intended us to. Just do your bit old son to make it happen. That will please me". He then said "Michael, when I die, you will find a box that I have kept in my attic for the last 45 years. In it you will find all the proof of what I have been telling you". I said "Dad don't talk like that, you're not going anywhere yet". It was then I asked him about after the war, about the things he had seen and been made to do, who did he tell these things to?. He replied "once I was taken to Rangoon and as they started to get me round and I started to put some weight on and felt that bit better, I was visited by someone from the war crimes investigations department of the war office. I can't remember his name but he was a very tall slim man and I remember

25

him saying that he had also been a prisoner of the Japanese. He questioned me for about three days and the things I have told you son are much the same as I told him. I told him the names of the Japanese guards and Officers that I knew had beaten my mates to death. The names I gave him did not seem to surprise him one bit, these were the names of the guards etc. that had been at the camps on the death railway. I think he already knew about these Japs – it was the ones that I could tell him about while I was in Singapore with the Executioner that he seemed more interested in".

"After those three days I never saw him again and I was soon on my way back to England on the hospital ship. I did follow the news of the war crimes back in England and was pleased to see that most of the Japs that I had seen inflicting such evil torture on fellow humans were put to death or given life imprisonment. I think after that Michael I tried to lock it all out and start a new life, for I was one of the lucky ones – I had come home. But try as I may to lock it out, it would always come back to me in my dreams at night. I know you remember only too well, son, the nights I woke you all up shouting out with my nightmares but I'm afraid it's been like that ever since I came home. I still have nightmares about it all even now, the only time I have really felt at ease, son, is when I have been in the company of my fellow comrades because I know that they all have suffered the same and you don't have to make any excuses to them, you can just relax and know that they understand". At this point I gave my dad a big hug and we sat and cried once more. What a couple we must have looked. I'm sure the nurses thought I was just a big cry baby but they did not know what we were talking about and I think it's enough to make anyone cry.

My dear dad's days were numbered now and not long after this long chat about the war he suffered a massive heart attack and was taken from us. His days of suffering were over and he was free at last. Although I and my family miss him so much, we know how lucky we were to have been blessed to have him for as long as we did. At the post mortem the head of the team that carried it out at King's Lynn Hospital told me it was just a miracle how he had got through the last 10 years as the worms had caused so much damage to his heart. I often think if only we had got him to see a doctor sooner he might still be here today. But then perhaps as I said earlier, it's all part of God's plan that we shall never understand. At my dad's funeral, I was so proud to read the bible passage over him that he had read so many times over those poor victims he had laid to rest in that mass grave, and all his poor mates that had died on the death railway. I then sang his favourite hymn 'Abide

26

with me'. I still shed a tear every time I hear it, for to me it was his hymn and when my day comes it's one I shall want sung at my own funeral.

After we all got back home after the funeral and all the guests had gone, my mother, my wife and I sat talking. We were worried about my son and daughter who were so distraught at the loss of their dear grandad. Their partners had taken them home and there was nothing we could do but worry how they were, for their grandad had been so much to them, it had hit them so hard. I think like me, they knew he would not be there for them any more, for yes, we all just took it for granted that grandad would know what to do but now that feeling that we were on our own came home to us all. I said to my mother "Mum, I am going to find that box that dad told me to look in, do you know just where it is?" she replied "yes I do Michael, but I have never seen in it". I said "well you will now mum, it's coming out of that attic for good". As I got up in the attic and came to where the box was, I just froze, for what was I to find in it? Would it unfold more nightmares than I could bare? But at the same time I knew I had to open it. I brought it down into the room and said to my wife and mother, "here we go then, this is the right time to do it. I feel dad would want us to look now. Yes, on the day of his funeral, while we are all so upset". I think they both agreed although they never said a thing.

I opened up the box and there was a piece of bamboo about 12" long x 2" round, it had been hollowed out and as I looked inside it I could see that there were papers inside. I carefully took them out and laid them on the table. We all looked at one another and there was total silence at that moment. I untied this small package of paper and there inside were six photos plus some old thin note paper that had been written on in very faint pencil. I knew at once that these were notes my father had risked his life to keep a record of those nightmare days he had been forced to endure at the hands of his Japanese captors. The writing had faded but I could make out some parts of the notes enough to know they were of friends my father had seen beaten to death. He had put down the dates and at what camp these atrocities had taken place and some of the names of the guards who had carried these things out. Then there were the six photos. As I looked at them I think it fair to say I was in a state of shock at what I was looking at. For they were some of the worst horrific photos I or anyone would ever be likely to see, the only one that was not horrific was the photo of the Executioner and some of the Japanese soldiers and my father with some of the other British prisoners that were used as drivers. I knew it had been taken at River Valley Camp soon after they had been sent to this Camp because my father had told me about it while sharing his nightmare stories with me while he was in Ely RAF Military Hospital. But the other five photos were the ones he wanted me to see and I knew now why he had told me where I would find the box and why I was to go to it once he was dead. He knew that once I saw these photos I would have all the proof of what he had shared with me was completely true.

As I sat and looked at these photos a cold shiver went right through me – the first one was of some young nurses in a state of undress. I knew they had been raped and murdered, I wondered to myself if these were some of those poor young nurses from the Alexandra Hospital massacre that had been a subject my father and I had discussed in depth. The photo I looked at next was of a dear tiny baby on the end of a Japanese soldiers bayonet. The next was of a young man who had been beheaded. I wondered to myself if this could have been the first young man that my father had seen beheaded – the one I shared with you in "My Dad My Hero". The next one was of some young Chinese that had been badly mutilated and beheaded. The next was of a man who had suffered the Japanese water treatment and he lay with his stomach split open – not a nice sight I can assure you. I knew then I could not let my mother see them in the state she was in, or my wife, so I just put them away and told them it would be better for them not to look at them now.

Over the next eight to 10 months my wife and I, with the help of magnifying glasses, were to sit most evenings carefully writing over my fathers notes, the stories that we were to unfold and the tears we shed are a thing our hearts and minds will never let us forget. It was one evening while doing this that my wife was to look at the photos. She then just fell into my arms and we both cried our eyes out, for my dad had been such a father to my wife as well as me and I knew just how much she loved him and missed him. I think it was that night we decided I must write a book about him to honour his memory and to raise funds for those brave FEPOWS still suffering from tropical worms in their blood and from the mental war trauma that comes back to haunt them in their old age.

My wife said "Mike, we can't use these photos in any book, they are just too horrific for people to see". So we decided to send them off to the Imperial War Museum for them to use as they think fit. I did use the one of the Executioner and one of the poor young man beheaded as many of you will know in my book "My Dad My Hero" – the book that started me off in my writing career.

I would like to share with you now just how that book was written. I had suffered an industrial accident and had damaged three spinal discs in my back and could not feel my legs properly. I had to lay flat on my back for six months before they could operate. After a short time like this you can imagine how bored I was getting. My son said "Dad I am going to make you a wooden lectern that will fit right over you and you must write that book you have promised to do about my grandad". As my son is a wood machinist I don't think it was too hard for him but I shall always be grateful to him for the part he played in helping me get started in the writing game. So you see my friends that's how "My Dad My Hero" was written. I have since had the three discs removed and with bits of metal in their place, I am now walking again and getting on quite well apart from the back ache.

I have made so many friends from FEPOWS that read "My Dad My Hero" which, as you know, was how my second book "Forgotten Heroes" came about. One dear friend who shared his story with us in that book is Robert Driver, one of my heroes. He has just loaned me a book to read called 'Cyril Wild – the tall man who never slept', written by James Bradley, a man who we shall hear about later in this book.

It is a book I would recommend to you. Major Cyril Wild who went on to become a full Colonel and suffered with his men at Sonkrai Camp. He spoke fluent Japanese and after the war he stayed behind to work with the war crimes department. Unfortunately he died in a plane crash while flying to Singapore from Hong Kong to attend the trial that would have meant so much to him – that of the Japanese Officers and guards from Sonkrai Camp. I wonder could this have been the tall slim man that interviewed my father? I feel sure it could have been and I just hope the things my father told him were able to help him to bring these barbarous Japs to their just ends.

As I sit writing this it is the day after Remembrance day and at this time a lot of debate is going on as whether we should observe the two minute silence. Well friends, I think it is a thing we must never let go even until the end of time. We owe these men and the men of all wars who have given their lives for our freedom that much, and I would ask in that two minutes silence, as we remember them, to just take in how lucky we are to have a life today for I know if the Nazis and those Japanese of the 40's had won the war we would not be here today.

I will remember my dear father every day of my life for I loved him so much and I know how privileged I am that he shared his stories with me before he went to meet his maker. God rest his soul.

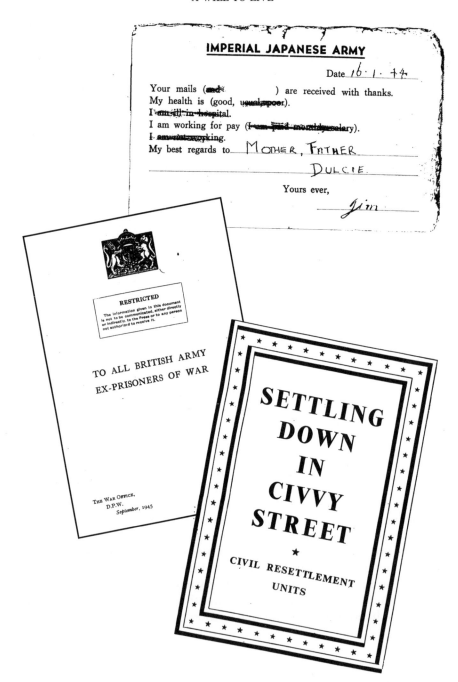

IMPERIAL JAPANESE ARMY

Date *16 · 1 · 44*

Your mails (~~and~~) are received with thanks.
My health is (good, ~~usual, poor~~).
~~I am ill in hospital.~~
I am working for pay (~~I am paid monthly salary~~).
~~I am not working.~~
My best regards to MOTHER, FATHER

DULCIE.

Yours ever,

Jim

TO ALL BRITISH ARMY
EX-PRISONERS OF WAR

THE WAR OFFICE,
D.P.W.
September, 1945

**SETTLING
DOWN
IN
CIVVY
STREET**

★

CIVIL RESETTLEMENT
UNITS

CHAPTER TWO

Stanley Chown's Story

I share with you now another true story from another of my heroes, a man with whom my wife and I have now become good friends. Many of you may remember him, he is Mr Stanley Chown MBE, and those of you that have read "Forgotten Heroes" may remember that Stanley's wife Dora wrote to me after she and Stanley had read "My Dad My Hero" to say how moved they were by it and to let me know that Stanley had been a Japanese prisoner of war. The letter was included in the letter section of "Forgotten Heroes". It is my privilege now to share with you Stanley's full story.

Stanley was born in 1911 at Fernlea Cottage, 6 Cavendish Avenue, Cambridge. The property was owned by Stanley's father's employer, a Mr Colin Lynn, who owned several tobacco shops in Cambridge at that time. Stanley's father was on the reserve from the Grenadier Guards so as soon as the first world war started he was called up. He saw some of the worst action of that campaign and in 1917 was badly wounded. He was hit in thirteen places but by some miracle he lived. He was bought back to London where he stayed in hospital for the next three years. Stanley's mother took Stanley and his elder brother to live in London with some of their relations that lived there so that she could be near to her husband. Whilst there, Stanley and his brother went to school but Stanley never forgot those days or the times he was allowed in to see his father because, unlike today, it was not allowed to let young children into the wards, so the odd times he was allowed to see his father meant so much to him. Once his father was able to leave hospital, they all returned to Cambridge and moved into a house in Blinco Grove. Here his mother and father were to spend the rest of their days. Stanley's father never did have all the shrapnel removed from his body and carried bits of it in him until the day he died.

Stanley attended Morley Memorial School which was also in Blinco Grove. Like all young boys he loved sport and excelled at football, making the school team and can even remember some of the goals he scored. Stanley enjoyed his young life and soon grew to be a fine young man. The war to end all wars had been fought, as Stanley knew only too well from his boyhood memories of that great war. Also by knowing that his dear father was still one of those suffering from it.

In 1926 Stanley started work as an apprentice chef at Pembroke College, Cambridge. In those days they were known as College Servants. There was great competition at all Colleges in football, cricket and rowing and Stanley soon found himself involved in all three. His memory of those days seemed to be as if it had been just yesterday. He told me how they would go off to Oxford to play their sister College, Queens, at cricket and then to partake of tea with them in the College grounds. One can imagine those happy summer days of enjoying life and Stanley told me how much he enjoyed them and of how much he owed those brave men that had fought for their country so that he and others could enjoy a free life. He told me how lucky he was to have such a good mother and father who saw to it that he got apprenticed to a good trade.

Although it was hard work and very long hours, he knew it was something he wanted to do and after months of doing all the dirty jobs the top chefs knew he had the stomach for it and soon had him working along with them, teaching him all they could. Stanley was quick to learn and was soon given responsibility at a young age, a thing that was to stand him in good stead for the years to come.

In 1930 Stanley met his true love as he says "my wonderful Dora". Over the next few years they enjoyed life together when they were not working and enjoyed life as young people should. They became engaged and had planned to marry but then the talk of war sprung up again and so they decided to wait. As you will see, over the next few years it was to be a long wait for Dora before she would be able to see and marry her true love, for the second world war had now begun. Those dark clouds had fallen across Europe once more and Stanley was called to do his bit for his country. When I say called I mean in Stanley's heart, for he did not wait to receive call up papers, he knew only too well it was his duty to offer his services to defend his country and so he took himself off to the Wesley Church in King Street, Cambridge where he knew they were recruiting. Even knowing the things he did of the nightmares war could bring, here he was in line waiting his turn to sign up. As he stood in this line his thoughts went back to the times his father had told him about his experiences of the first world war and Stanley knew only too well how it had affected his fathers life but as he told me, even though he knew all this, his heart was telling him this is what you must do. As he stood there with these thoughts going through his mind, he was soon brought back to reality when a big Recruitment Sergeant bellowed in his ear, "sign here please". Stanley was soon back in the real world and once he had signed up and explained to them what his trade was, he was told by one of the Officers to apply to be a

Warrant Officer in the catering company. Stan thought about this but decided he could serve his country better by being where the action was to be and so he joined the 196 Field Ambulance Regiment. Over the next few weeks before Stanley had to report at Aldershot Army Barracks, he took time to visit his friends to say his goodbyes, and to say his farewell to his beloved Pembroke College and all his workmates.

The Master of the College shook him by the hand and told him "it won't be long, Stanley, before you are back here with us old son. We shall be thinking of you and you will be in our prayers and before you know it, you will be back here with us". He said to Stanley "remember all you have learnt here and put it to good use". With a gentle tear running down his cheek, Stanley turned and walked out of Pembroke College wondering in his heart if he would ever be back there again, for in the few years Stanley had been working for the College, he had already fallen in love with it. He loved his job, he loved playing football, cricket and his rowing for the College but now these were to be put on hold – just happy memories to carry with him over the next six years.

The day soon came to leave home and Stanley said his goodbyes to his parents and brother and then to his darling Dora. As he held her in his arms, he asked her to wait for him. She told him, "Stanley, wherever you are, my heart is yours, my love will always be with you until the end of time. Wherever you are at night, just look up at that big old moon and think of me darling, and know that my love for you will help you through". They then kissed and said their goodbye.

Stanley was now on his own as he set off but not for long – as he boarded the train to take him to Aldershot, there were many more young men doing just the same as him. They soon got chatting to one another and struck up friendships which were to help them all get through their training together. The powers that be soon saw how good a cook he was and after taking all the tests they could throw at him, which Stanley passed with flying colours, he soon found himself cooking for Officers – something that would help him in the years to come.

Stanley was soon sent to Norton Hall in Wales and also to Scotland but the day soon came when his unit was to join the 18th Division and set off for the Far East, although Stanley had no idea of where they were off to at that time. On a foggy day they set off to join the convoy to start their journey into the unknown. Once they got to Iceland and Greenland they were met by an American Fleet which showed a very impressive display of strength. They were to escort Stanley and his comrades to Halifax, Nova Scotia, in Canada. Here they were all transferred to American transportation and Stanley was put aboard the Joseph T

"U.S.S. Joseph T. Dickman"

Christmas Dinner

1941

AT SEA, NORTH INDIAN OCEAN.

Menu

Roast Turkey

Giblet Gravy   Sage Dressing
Pickles   Cranberry Sauce
Mashed Potatoes
Buttered Peas

Plum Pudding   Camperdown Sauce
Fruit Salad

Bread   Butter
Tea
Candy   Raisin Cookies   Cigarettes

Dickman. At this time America had not entered the war against the Japanese and Stanley found out the ship he was on was an old coast guard ship. They soon reached Trinidad, Cape Town and after five days of sight seeing they were off to India and Armangar for intensive training. While here Stanley was to find out that they were now off to defend Singapore at post haste. Stanley was put aboard Miss America, later to be called West Point, the ship on which my own dear father had arrived at Singapore. Stanley told me how they were bombed on the way by enemy aircraft but thankfully none of them hit the West Point. Stanley told me "at that time they must have been bad shots but they had improved by the time we arrived at Singapore. As we tried to leave the ship, the docks were taking a severe bombing and many men lost their lives".

In the next six weeks Stanley was to see all over the island setting up his kitchens and soon was promoted to Corporal. He knew only too well how important it was to keep the men well fed but being so close to the action had very bad effects on ones cooking. "Things like a mortar bomb hitting the kitchen could send your pots flying let alone take someone's life. It was very hard work as well, but a badly fed army could not be expected to fight, so we all knew how important our job was. When the General of the 18th Division was to pay a visit to one of our cooking stations, someone from HQ would ring to say he was coming but you no sooner put the 'phone down and he was there. This was always the case with us of the 196 Regiment but we usually had a good display of food to show him. My cooks, like myself, were all so very good and worked very hard at this time. On one of these occasions, the General said to me 'how do you know when I am coming to visit you?' My Colonel, who was present, replied 'oh this is a daily thing for Sergeant Chown Sir, we always have very splendid dishes every day Sir." The General said "Sergeant Chown, where did you learn to cook such wonderful dishes?" Stanley proudly replied, "at Pembroke College, Cambridge, Sir" to which the General replied "I know why now". He then patted Stanley on the head and said "I was at Trinity myself laddie, so I know now how lucky your men are to have someone with your training, keep up the good work laddie". Stanley told me he likes to think he and his fellow cooks did just that right up to the time of surrender.

Stanley told his Colonel how he had called him Sergeant Chown to which the Colonel replied "yes, Chown, that's what you are now. I will take care of the paperwork, you just see to it that other stripe gets put on". It was now near to mid February 1942 and Stanley knew only too well that the Japanese were taking control of Singapore island. He was one of the first to know that the water had been turned off and instructed his men to be extra careful in preparing the food, "the last thing we want is an outbreak of dysentery", a thing that Stanley and the others were to become so used to over the next three and a half years.

Then came that fateful day, Sunday 15th February 1942, a day Stanley and his comrades will never forget. Stanley saw the white flag hoisted by General Percival that day at Fort Canning. And as the surrender party left, Stanley saw Captain Cyril Wild holding the white flag of surrender – the same Cyril Wild that I believe interviewed my own father after the war. With him were Brigadier K S Torrance, Brigadier T K Newbigging and Lieutenant General A E Percival. They were met by Lieutenant Colonel Ichiji Sugita, Intelligence Officer, 25th Imperial Japanese Army and Lieutenant Hishikari, Imperial Japanese Army Interpreter. They were met on the Bukittimah Road and taken to the Ford Motor Factory where the surrender was to take place. As we now know, ammo had run out and already many men had died in the hand to hand fighting that was taking place, where men were prepared to fight to the death. I have told you before that all the FEPOWS I have spoken to were quite prepared to give their lives in this way. Much is made of the Japanese Kamikaze pilots giving their lives but many of our own men gave their lives in a last attempt to save their positions when their ammo had ran out. Those heroes who were to give up their lives in this way were to be spared the next three and a half years of living hell – no consolation to their families though.

Many of you will know that Captain Wild was able to hide the Union Jack flag and on many occasions when asked by the Japanese where it was, he would tell them that he had burnt it on the day of surrender, while looking towards England, and this the Japanese always believed. The flag was to be used many times at the funerals of our boys on the death railway and today it is on display at the late Colonel Wild's school chapel at Charterhouse.

For Stanley and his comrades the war was now over and hell on earth was just beginning for them, although none of them knew what to expect. By this time many of them had heard the rumours of the Alexandra Hospital massacre; also they had heard of what the Japanese had been doing to the Chinese in China for the last few years. The thoughts that were going through Stanley's head now were are these rumours true? What will they do to us now that we have surrendered? Stanley was soon to find out the next day, when the Japanese rounded up Stanley and his comrades and marched them off to a submarine base. Once here Stanley soon made himself busy setting up a kitchen but little did he know then that the Japanese would not be allowing him to cook the dishes he was used to cooking. Yes, over the next three and a half years Stanley was to become an expert on rice dishes. He told me with a smile how the men's favourite greeting on meeting another FEPOW over those three and a half years was "turned out rice again'.

After a short time here Stanley was sent to Changi Prison where he was to be cook. He was very surprised to find that he and the other cooks were allowed to make their way to Changi in an old cooks lorry and even more surprised to find it still was loaded with food, something he felt sure the Japanese would have not allowed if they had known about it. The food was quickly unloaded and hidden on arrival at Changi and Sergeant Chown was made NCO in charge of the kitchen for the Hospital personnel, plus about 100 Cambridgeshire's. The extra food from the lorry was to prove a real life saver for those poor sick lads who had been wounded in the last few days of the action or those that had gone down with sickness. Stanley told me he was cooking for up to 2,000 men now and while rations lasted he even made puddings and was soon given the name Sergeant Duff. He did not mind this one bit for it gave his men something to boost their morale. Many of the men were now working each day in work parties around Singapore and often brought Stanley food that they had bartered for with the locals or had stolen. Stanley told me "I can't stress to you enough the bravery of these men Michael, for they were not thinking of themselves but of their poor friends in Hospital huts. On many occasions food would just appear. I did not always know who had risked their life to get it, I only knew they wanted it to go to those poor lads in the Hospital and I was only too pleased to play my part in preparing it for them".

After some months at Changi, owing to lack of food and water, dysentery was taking a hold on most of the men. Stanley was very strict with his men that they must maintain cleanliness at all times. They were already boiling all water and scrubbing their hands raw to try and prevent any contamination coming from their kitchen but the problem was the thousands of flies. Stanley told me "the problem was we were so close to the Hospital and too near the dysentery wards and those flies carried so many germs. I knew to prepare food under these conditions was not right but my pleas for help to the Japanese fell on deaf ears, all I would receive from them was a clout around the head and be told 'you prisoner, you no say what you want Japanese to do, *we* tell *you* what to do' followed by another clout". One day Stanley was chatting to one of the Officers that he cooked for – James Bradley, an RE Officer. Stanley told him of the conditions he and his men were having to cook in and felt sure the flies were causing a lot of the trouble and adding to the dysentery epidemic at Changi. He told him what the Japanese had told him and showed him the bruise to show what their reply had been. The Officer replied "Stanley, don't worry. I think I have the answer to your problem. I have found an old dump on the outskirts of town and I know that in it are many old mosquito nets. If I can get them back here and into camp, I think I can help you with the problem". The two men then shook hands and went on about their duties.

Over the next few days Stanley saw mosquito nets arriving en mass. Officer James Bradley had saved the day. He and his men built Stanley a fly-proof room out of the nets. Stanley made this the prep room and every bit of food was now prepared in here. Stanley told me "it was a wonderful place to work, you could see all the thousands of flies trying to get in at you but they never did. I know this helped our dysentery epidemic and know how much we owed James Bradley at that time.

Over the next year Stanley was to see many nightmares unfold at Changi, he saw scenes that only those there will only ever know the real nightmare of. Yes, things that still bring a tear to him when he recalls them to mind, like the time he saw a young comrade knocked to the floor by one of the Jap guards by a rifle butt in the face, just because the Jap felt he had not bowed to him as he should. Once down on the ground the guard was joined by other guards who took great delight in kicking the poor chap to death. I know it is things like this that Stanley and his comrades can never forgive or forget for as I have said many times it was just murder. Stanley told me of how you never had to do anything wrong to receive the Japs brutality, just being in the wrong place at that time was all it took and if the guards took a dislike to you, you were as good as dead – a thing that was to come home to Stanley even more in the next two and a half years. He was to see some of the worst things imaginable to mankind.

It was now 1943 and rumours were running around the camp that 196 Field Ambulance was to be moved to Thailand to proper Red Cross camps. As one Jap told Stanley, "you soon be going to holiday camps, you have good time, much food you cook, whatever you want". Stanley went to sleep that night feeling much happier than he had for a long time. He hoped and prayed it was to be true for he felt even he could not go on much longer like this, for he had already had several malaria attacks and his share of dysentery. As he slept his dreams were of his darling Dora and family back home. He knew it was one way to escape the nightmare he was in, as he dreamed of those happy times back home with his loved ones, a thing he told me he never let go of, for he still believes it was these dreams that gave him the strength to carry on each day. He was soon awoken in the early hours of the morning by someone prodding at him, his natural instinct was to roll into a ball as all prisoners soon learnt to do, fearing it to be a Japanese guard. But as he looked up, he saw it was a fellow prisoner of war. who said to him "don't worry Sergeant, it's only me". Stanley could see that it was one of Colonel Huston's men. He told Stanley "the Colonel wants to see you as soon as possible". Stanley pulled his boots on and said "no time like the present, let's go". As he came before the Colonel, Stanley joked to him "what's up Sir, do you want me to prepare you an early breakfast?" to which came a sharp reply "no Sergeant Chown I do not. I want you and your men to get everything ready to move. I have put your name on the list to go with F Force to go up to Thailand, you have worked wonders here Chown, you deserve a break. I know only too well that many of our men would not have come this far without your cooking and your kindness. The Japanese have told me that they are building proper Red Cross camps and are moving our men to them now. I know they will need a good cook and so I am letting you go with them so go and get your men to prepare everything ready to move". Stanley spent the day getting all the things they could carry ready to set off on their best promise yet. Men were joking to one another of how good it would be: many said how they would soon put on weight once Stanley and the other cooks received better food to cook for them, but Stanley had seen enough of the Japanese not to believe anything until he saw it with his own eyes. He and his men joined the long line of men on their march to the station. After being made to stand in the full heat of the sun for some hours they were finally marched off. Stanley told me "we looked a sorry lot, the stronger ones helping those that could not manage under their own steam. After some hours we arrived at the station where most

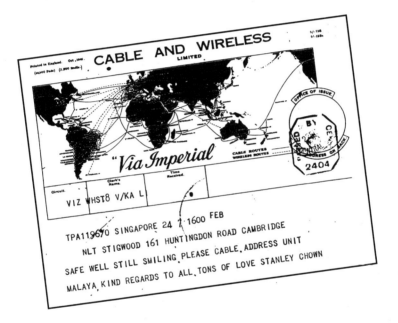

of the cooking utensils that we were carrying were taken from us, the Japanese told us we would not need them as all cooking would be done in new camps with all new equipment.

It was then I feared the worst as we were loaded into steel sided cattle trucks, thirty men to a truck – some of the trucks had more than this. It was so very hot and I was very worried about those men in my truck that were already ill. Most of us had dysentery and some had malaria. We had very little water and this is what worried me most, knowing as I did how important it was to keep our fluid intake going in such heat. It seemed like hours before we set off and once under way we tried to cheer one another up by saying "it won't be long now before we can eat and drink much better. Once we get to these new red cross camps we will soon get better". One chap said "yeah, I heard from me mum that me brother who is a prisoner of the Germans receives real big Red Cross parcels, so you see once we get them, we will be fine". Stanley told me he took this in like water off a ducks back as seeing is believing and from what he had seen of the Japs promises so far, they had not been any good at all. He told his men "don't build your hopes up too much lads, just look at the transport they have provided for us", to which came the reply "yes but at least we have not got to walk". That evening came their first stop for food and drink. The food was one pint of rice slop per man. They were informed this was to be made to last them all day and if they were lucky they received a little dried fish. The water was taken from the river and Stanley and his fellow cooks would boil it up, those men who had such a craving thirst they could not wait for it to be boiled were to be the ones to suffer even worse dysentery and sickness as the river water was so infected.

After some five and a half days like this they arrived at the first camp Ban Pong. Those that had believed what the Japanese had told them were soon to find out different. The few huts that were there were in a terrible state, with large holes in the roofs and you were up to your knees in thick black mud. There was raw sewage floating on top of this mud and once again there were flies everywhere. Everyone knew now that things were even worse than they had left behind at Changi. Many men just broke down and gave up for they had built themselves up so much to believe that after a year of suffering that at last it was to be over, but as Stanley told me "the only ones that it was over for was those who had not made the journey. Because it was so wet everywhere they had to be buried on high ground – the only problem with this was that if the camp had a well, the water that ran over their decaying bodies would end up in the well and cause even more illness. Many men spent that night sleeping up to their waists in this mud and slime, most of them in a state of shock, not knowing what was to become of them.

The next morning they were rounded up and counted, then the Japanese Commandant informed them that they were here to build a railway. They would be under orders from Japanese Engineers and must obey all orders, anyone who does not will be punished by death. "You are not going to stay here, you go to start work on camps and railway at Sonkari, you must march there but you be alright, Japanese guards take care of you, no wild animals hurt you, you all be OK". Stanley knew now that things were going to get even worse, as he said, it was not wild animals that worried him but the Japanese guards that he believed could act worse than any wild animal, a thing that Stanley and his comrades were to find out was true over the next year only too well. It was around midday when they departed from Ban Pong. Stanley told me "it was a sight I will never forget – men that could hardly stand were now expected to march over 200 miles to Sonkari. Around 1,650 men left camp Ban Pong that day to start this nightmare march. It was the monsoon season and the rainfall was very fast. Men were slipping over even as they stood in line waiting to leave the camp. As usual the Japanese kept them standing in line waiting for a few hours, as was the norm now. When at last they did set off the sun was starting to fall fast and they were soon marching by moonlight. They arrived at some old huts after marching along for about five hours, here they were allowed to rest for what was left of the night – most of the men just fell asleep through sheer exhaustion. But at first light they were awoken and after a cup of soup that was more like muddy water they set off again. By that evening they had arrived at Kanburi camp now known as Kanchanburi. This was about 55 miles from Ban Pong and most of the men were in a bad way from heat exhaustion. This camp is now well known as many of you will know for its famous bridge, the bridge over the river Kwai. From now on their march would be through virgin jungle for Kanburi was to be the last real place of civilisation that the men would see for the next year at least, those that were going to make it that is. The men were allowed to rest up now for a day and were informed that they would be leaving at night as all marching was to be done at night now to avoid the full heat of the day. Was this a goodwill gesture from the Japanese or a plea from the British Officers? Many rumours spread that day about this – many men believed it was to stop any allied planes from spotting them, others believed it would be so that the men could not see how many men were being killed because they could not keep up. Stanley told me "that day was just so full of rumours that one had to just believe what he thought best for himself". Stanley got as much rest as he could that day and as soon as the sun went down he was in line and ready to go with everything that he had to his name strapped to his back. The march soon got underway. Stanley believed they were following an old elephant track, and for the first few miles it was not too bad as the men had been allowed a full days rest and this had restored their strength a little but now that strength was waning, men were slipping over in the downpour of heavy rain. If their friends could not get them up quickly enough then the Jap guards were only too pleased to put the boot in or give them a rifle butt in the face to put them out. Orders came down the line from the British Officers to help one another all they could. As Stanley looked around him on hearing this order he could see only too well that the men were already doing this – many of the men were dragging a friend along with the help of another fitter man. They would help a friend along between them in the hope that with him in the middle of them it would keep the Jap guards from picking on him. They marched on like this all through the night and as the sun came up they could see through the morning mist a large mountain range on the horizon. Stanley thought to himself could it be these mountains that they were heading for? If it was, he knew it was going to take them weeks to make it and as this thought went through his head, he also thought to himself for the first time, I will never make it. I feel all in now and I have only been on the march for two days. As he was locked in thought like this he was soon brought back to life by a Jap guard's rifle digging him in the ribs and shouting at him "Speedo, you keep up". He took in a deep breath and put his best foot forward and locked his mind on his sweetheart back home.

He told himself "I will make it, I will come through this and get back home to her again". As he told me, it was to be these thoughts that would get him through the pain. Before he knew it, the order came to stop and after some rice slop, dried fish and a cup of muddy water, he settled down to sleep. He could see that those men suffering from dysentery were now in a very bad way and he feared for their safety. He drifted in and out of sleep that day as the sun was so hot and you just had to keep taking on water; also the moans and groans of the sick men did not allow you much rest.

Before they knew it the sun had set and they were off again into the unknown. They passed by Chungkai and Tamarkan crossing and it was now that they could see the first sign of the work on the railway. They could see and hear the rock blasting going on at Chungkai as the men there were cutting their way through a mountain pass, known as the Chungkai cutting. Stanley told me how perhaps my own dear father was there at that time. He told me the crossing at Tamarkan was very dangerous as the monsoon had swollen the river so much it was running at such fast speed and some of the weaker men slipped and met their end here. It was here that Stanley and many of the others knew that they could not carry the items on their backs anymore – no way could they cross this river with such weight on their backs to hold them down. The Japanese did not give them time to carry out any other method of getting their belongings across and so it was that many items that would have been so valuable in the days ahead were just left.

The men could see floodlights blazing out and knew that the prisoners at these camps were being made to work through the night. The men said to one another "what's the use if we do survive this so called march, these bloody Japs are only going to work us to death". Stanley told his men "try not to think like that lads, just take each day as it comes and give thanks that you get through it, think of the good things in life and they will help you overcome this evil". As the days and nights went by Stanley knew he was getting much weaker and he could see that it was now not a march but more like a bunch of stragglers. He saw many of his friends that could not keep up meet their end from one of these hateful guards. He told me "it was survival of the fittest now. Those who could not keep up, you just did not see again. You knew what had been their fate as when you started to drop behind there was always that Jap guard to remind you of what would happen to you if you could not keep up. I was one of the lucky ones and always found some inner strength from somewhere. We came to Wampo where the now famous viaducts are built and here our track ended and the foothills began. We had to cross over the viaducts, not a very nice thing to do in the dark. As we stepped over each sleeper you could hear the raging river below and once again some of the men were to go on no further, for them it was to be a watery grave. Those that did fall to their deaths like this were not always to blame for their fall as the Jap guards with us did not worry who they pushed – if they themselves slipped they would grab hold of whatever they could to save themselves and if a poor innocent prisoner got knocked over instead this was no worry to them, for we knew by now that our lives meant nothing to them at all.

As we left Wampo the journey was now to be even worse. The rain was so hard and fast it made it so hard to stand. Men were now so weak that not much talking was done, just the call of 'mind that branch, watch out for that drop, watch that bamboo'. These warnings were passed back whenever we could for if you cut yourself it would turn septic and the end result could be the loss of an arm or leg or even death so we all appreciated these warnings between one another".

Stanley told me how he remembered arriving at one camp which he believed to be Tarsau where the Camp Commandant looked just like Hitler even though he was Japanese. The other terrible thing was that he based his life on the same lines as Hitler, he even had a small black Hitler-like moustache. The thing Stanley remembered most of this hateful man was that he had a bad limp.

The men were allowed their day's rest here but no one could rest

43

much for fear of this Jap Commandant who made it clear he only wanted them there if they were to be put to work on his part of the railway. Stanley and the others were only too pleased when evening came and they could get away from him and his brutal ways, for that day they had seen many prisoners beaten to near death by him. As they set off there was no talking now, just every man deep in his own thoughts, saving all his strength for what was to come.

They had not gone far when men were starting to drop through sheer exhaustion. A dear friend of Stanley's, a man I have mentioned before in my books, was to set the example needed at this time to save these poor men. Yes, the late Canon Duckworth, a man with a heart as big as an elephant – and where he got his strength from at that time Stanley will never know. For he picked up men who had fallen and carried them in his arms until they had rested a little and could try to make it on their own again, for he knew if they were just left it would be that Jap bayonet for them. Many men followed his example and picked their friends up to save them from that Jap bayonet. Stanley had known Padre Duckworth from his days at College and had followed his rowing career – he had been the Cox of the Cambridge boat in 1933, 1934 and 1935, a thing Stanley would have loved to have done. Padre Duckworth took many a beating from the Japanese in his attempts to help those worse off than himself in those nightmare days and his memory will live on forever in the hearts of all FEPOWS.

Stanley told me "by now my boots had fallen to bits and so I had to discard them and go on bare footed, a thing that many of the others were now doing". Stanley found out that his Officers had pleaded in vain with the Japanese to leave their sick men at the next camp as they could just not keep up. This was denied them and those poor men were to die on the march and be left to rot in this hell hole of a jungle. With a gentle tear Stanley told me he could never forget their faces as they dropped to the ground, knowing it was to be their end for they had chosen the bayonet instead of the pain of life going on around them – for them it was over. Stanley told me how he lost many of his friends like this – "they were just like walking skeletons, as we all were by now and it was only my thoughts of my loved ones back home that spurred me on. On the odd occasion that we passed some isolated village we could some-times manage to get some fresh water and fruit from the locals but by now we had no valuables to barter with so we had to rely on the kind-ness of these natives".

They knew how important it was to boil the water and Stanley could remember how he had burnt his mouth because he was so thirsty that he had gulped down this boiling water so fast for fear of a Jap guard spotting the natives helping them.

It was only now that the column stretched out so long that the guards could not always see what was happening. Stanley told me "our column stretched out for miles and these natives would just appear from nowhere. It was this fruit and fresh water that was to save many of us at this time". Stanley told me of all the people to help them it was mainly the Chinese who did it without wanting anything in return. He felt sure that even in this God-forsaken hell hole those Chinese had heard of what the Japanese had been doing to their own people over the last eight years and felt sure that is why they were only too pleased to help any prisoner of the Japanese if they could. Some of the men who were dying were even taken by these Chinese at very great risk and we now know that many men were restored to health and kept hidden by the Chinese to survive the war. But for Stanley it was onwards ever onwards..... as daybreak came he would fall to the ground. Once the column had been bought to a halt the first thing he would do then was to tend to his blisters, there were no bandages and so he would wrap them in jungle leaves for the day in the hope that it would help them from ulcerating. Many of the men were now suffering from badly ulcerated legs and the smell of them was something Stanley can never forget.

Then after a short rest he would help prepare the rice slop. He and his fellow cooks would throw in anything they could from the jungle that they thought would be safe to eat just to try and make it that bit more wholesome for the men. Stanley had now been hit by another attack of malaria and so he was only too pleased to get what rest he could. He could not remember the next few days or nights only to say that it was his turn to owe his life to his friends for helping him survive those days and drag him along and protect him from the Jap guards. He told me of how much he owed his friends for if it had not been for them he knew only too well how it would have been the bayonet for him. Once he was that bit better he could not thank them enough for he knew that they had enough to do to carry themselves along. He knew that he could never repay them for keeping him alive, he gave thanks to God for them that day and knowing how lucky he had been made him all the more determined to get through this nightmare. He now did all he could to help anyone who could not keep up and being in the 196 Field Ambulance Regiment he found himself towards the back of the column with the medical boys trying to administer any help they could give to those suffering from leg ulcers, dysentery, malaria etc. It was here that Stanley saw many deaths as the Japanese would not allow them time to rest and have their wounds seen to, they would just push the medics out of the way and administer the bayonet. Stanley saw even some of the Officers suffer like this as they begged for mercy for these men, a thing he never forgets. He told me "it is these sights you see every day in your mind Michael, it can hit you at any time, just a flash back and you are in a cold sweat when sights like that are imprinted on your mind, you can never forget them.

Now an even more evil death was to be among them – cholera. As they passed camps where the natives were working they had come into contact with it, for the natives had not bothered to dig proper latrines and the men had been made to march through human droppings that were infected with blood; flies were everywhere and the fear of one landing on your mouth was sure to bring death. If any of these flies landed on your rice ration you had to throw it away and go without even though you were starving. The water was boiled so much it evaporated, for this was the fear that cholera had brought to the men. No one dare risk putting their feet into the river to ease them, such was the fear of death from cholera, for you see the natives at this time did not have the sense to burn their cholera victims, they just threw them into our life-line, the river, and so cholera was to spread like an epidemic right along the length of the camps, just one of the reasons they were known as death camps.

The men had been on this forced march now for about two and a half weeks and Stanley told me he believed this camp they were now at to be Konquita, a camp built for coolie labour. "These coolies just lay dying all over the place – it was just sheer degradation. We thought we had arrived finally in hell. As we stepped over these dying people it went through my mind just why were the Japs making us suffer like this? Our Officers pleaded with the Camp Commandant to let us move on at once but to no avail. Needless to say no one got any rest that day and when evening came, most of us were only too pleased to be moving on. The damage had been done though, and the cholera death was to take many of our men from now on. We marched on like this for another week until at last we reached the first of Sonkari camps. We had now covered over 200 miles in the last three and a half weeks and those of us left alive knew what a miracle it was that we had made it. As men were taken from the column to stay at this camp, we said our goodbyes to our friends that were to stay there, then it was off again until we arrived at the next camp called Naka. Once again men were pulled from the column, I found myself still in the column and by now I was nearly done for. I knew the malaria had hit me again but feared it could be cholera. Had I come all this way to die like this in this God forsaken place? I don't remember much of that last part of the march until I heard the cry 'all men stop'. I fell to the ground and when I came to some hours later I was laid out in what was to be our medical hut. The medic informed me that I had a bad attack of malaria. He had no sooner told me this when two Jap guards arrived shouting 'all men come work now'. The medic told them that we are all sick men for which he received a smack in the face from a rifle butt and told 'no work, no food'. I don't know how I did it Michael, but I somehow pulled myself up and got outside in the line for work. Many of the others could not even get up, they were in such a bad way I was not to see them again, but for them the pain was now over. I was marched off with the others and put to work on clearing jungle growth ready for the railway. I know I only got through it with the help of the others around me and when they helped me back to camp that night, as we entered camp there was a large pile of our dead, waiting for cremation – this was to become a daily sight for us all. It was nothing to say goodnight to your chum next to you at night and then wake in the morning to find him lay there dead and then when you returned from work that evening to see his body on the pile of dead. You never ever forget those sights Michael, they live on with you for as long as you live."

"One day while I was working on the railway, our Major came along and shouted to me 'Sergeant Chown, why are you here?', to which I replied 'good question Sir. Why are any of us here? To build this damn railway for these Japs, I think Sir.' 'No, no, Chown' the Major replied, 'why are you not in our kitchens? When I think of all the good work you did to help our sick and dying back at Singapore, I know that you must be in our kitchen here, now, even if only in an advisory capacity. You leave it with me Chown, I will get this sorted out' ". The next day Stanley was taken off the railway work and put into the camp kitchens. Stanley told me with a tear that he knows this saved his life – at that time he was suffering from a very badly swollen foot that he feared would turn gangrenous. With this he was to be lucky, for he had made friends with an Australian Sergeant who lanced it for him and removed the poison. Another friend, an Indian Army Assistant Surgeon, helped as well by letting Stanley have some iodine which helped it to improve. The Australian Sergeant even ripped the sleeves from his shirt to use as bandages for him. "That's friendship," Stanley told me "and I know how much I owe them for helping me at that time. I was now back in my domain, a kitchen, albeit just an old jungle hut. I was able to do what I loved best, cooking. I knew that the normal rice slop we were given would not sustain for much longer as men were dying so fast now. I learnt to do things with rice that most people would not believe possible and I made a real meal from anything that could be caught from the jungle. My snake and rat stew was a great favourite with the men and for those too sick to eat, I prepared a light broth of anything I could obtain with some life-saving vitamins. The things I had bought to me to try and cook you would not believe but cook it I did and that was what was to keep us alive at that time".

"Things were getting so bad at Sonkari now that morale was at an all time low, the Officers knew something had to be done before we were all dead and so my Captain Anker and James Bradley and some other very brave men decided that they would plan an escape [read James Bradley's book 'Towards the Setting Sun']. I was kept in the dark about the escape until the day that the escape party decided to go, such was the fear of the Japanese finding out. For those involved it would have been certain death and I think it fair to say that James Bradley and his fellow Officers and men of the escape party knew this only too well, hence the need for such secrecy. It was only on the day of the escape that I was informed that I would be required to sleep in the kitchen that night so as to take the place of one of the escape party and not cause suspicion to the Japs. I kept my head very well covered so that the Japs did not recognise me that day, I can tell you".

"I had an idea something was afoot anyway, and I had taken the risk beforehand to steal some rice from the Jap cook store. This was kept on raised bamboo slats above the ground, so a good sharp knife cutting along the bottom of the sack allowed about a third of a sack to be spilled on to the floor. The cut was made in the bottom sack well to the back so that the Jap storeman could not see it on the floor. I would collect it up and use it for more food for our poor sick lads. I kept these things to myself but I had one close shave and as I returned to my hut my pal Haggy said 'you look like you have seen a ghost Stan'. I told him what I had done and he said 'you must be daft. You're crackers to try such things, it's far too risky'. My kitchen was near to the Officers hut and many of the Jap guards had been up to Burma on leave and they had brought back some chickens which they kept under the Jap Officers' hut. When they wanted one killed they would ask me to kill it for them and prepare it. On one occasion I killed one for myself and just as I had done this one of the guards turned up. My heart was really pumping then as I feared my end was nigh but he just grinned and said 'good man, you kill chickens for us' and walked off. I don't think I could have answered him anyway as I could not speak for fear. I took the other chicken for myself and for my sick pals. Haggy had his share and they all said how much it improved their rice that night. Yes, it had been worth taking the risk.

I knew how important the escape was, for the outside world had to know of how we were being treated before we all died and there was no one left to tell the truth of our treatment at Sonkari. I think just myself, a chap called Sayers (who was Captain Anker's Batman and one of the escape party) and our Regimental Quartermaster Sergeant John Franks were the only ones that knew anything about the escape. They, being very brave men, risked their lives to get food out of the Japanese stores". Stanley told me how "I shall never forget the fear in my heart on the occasion the Japanese store keeper walked in while I was busy stealing food for the escape party. Thank God he never saw me – and how he never heard my heart beating I shall never know, for it was nearly jumping out of my chest, such was my fear of being caught, which would of course have meant the abandoning of the whole escape. As I hid the food, I knew how lucky I had been and such was the secretive nature of the escape that I did not even tell anyone about it for fear of the Japs overhearing. I sat that evening and wrote a letter to my sweetheart Dora and my family, and these letters were carried by the escape party. Oh how I prayed they would make it to safety and that my darling Dora would receive word from me at last. I did not know for certain what was happening in the outside world at that time, and in my heart I hoped and prayed that they would be our saviours and get us out of this living hell". Stanley looked at me and with sadness in his eyes he said "you know the outcome of that, Michael, and to this day I hold them as the bravest men I have ever known". As I allowed Stanley time to compose himself a grin came over his face and he said "after the escape I never knew that I could tell so many lies, may God forgive me. I was soon taken by the Japanese and asked if I had supplied food for the escapees. They knew that food was missing from their store and must have known I knew about it, but my life was at stake and I told so many lies to them that I think in the end I was as shocked as they were when I was allowed to live".

"After this I was moved to cook just for Officers and the very nasty Jap guard put in charge of my cook house was a very hateful little man who took great delight in hitting me whenever he felt like it and telling me that I was 'a very bad man, no good man'. The Japanese had lost face over this escape – to lose prisoners like this would bring disgrace on them from their Emperor, for they had let him down. It didn't matter how many of us they killed – that was all right. But to have someone

49

escape from them was just unthinkable".

"Things were getting so bad now that all the Japs wanted was to get the railway finished so that they could get their troops up to Burma and which meant that men were having to work even harder and longer hours. This put our death rate at an all time high. The Japanese brought in several elephants, all female, to pull down the trees. One day a wild bull elephant, looking so very dangerous, came after them. Somehow the Japs managed to catch him and he was tethered outside the entrance to camp. We had to pass him every day and were so afraid of him as we were so weak we knew if he got loose it would be lights out for us. The one thing we did have in common with him was that we, like him, wanted to be free from our Japanese captors. What his fate was I can't say – one morning he was just not there anymore. I can't say I was sorry to see him gone".

"When you went to the latrines, you had to shout 'Bengo', and on your return 'Bengo Wodee'. If not, you received a bashing from a guard's rifle butt, often coming right in the middle of your back out of nowhere. On one particular evening as I was shouting this out, one of the guards came out of the darkness. I jumped back fearing a bashing but to my amazement he said 'you all go soon, back to Singapore'. As I walked back to my hut I did not dare tell any of the others in case it was another lie. I soon forgot this news when another attack of malaria took me over. It was to be one of my worst attacks and I thought it was my end as I lay there for days slipping in and out of consciousness. I remembered something my dear father had told me when I had been a young boy and had visited him in hospital. He told me 'old soldiers don't die they just fade away'. He even used to sing it to me sometimes and as I lay there I thought of those times all those years ago as a young lad. I wondered now was I to fade away? The thing the Jap guard had told me kept going through my mind.... 'All men go Singapore soon'.... could it be true? I knew I had to find strength from somewhere to get better, for if it *was* true I wanted to be back there more than anything – Changi had been a holiday camp compared to this place. I told myself I would get better and thanks to my determination and the help of our medics I came through it again. I can't remember just how many attacks of malaria I suffered as a prisoner but even now I still get mild attacks".

"It was not long after I got better that the news was given that we would be returning to Singapore, a thing all the men were so pleased to hear. I can still hear the cheer that went up. One of the men had a wireless hidden in our cholera ward and he told us how the allies were now winning the war! Oh how I prayed it was true. Was I soon to be free? I just did not dare think about it.... take each day as it comes, I told myself. Over the next few days we held our own remembrance services for our dear departed friends we were having to leave behind. Padre Duckworth said some very special words over these brave men and as the sound of the last post died away I can still hear the words "we will remember them", a thing I knew I would do every day for the rest of my life".

"The day soon came when we were to leave this living hell camp, for that's just what it was Michael, no other words for it. We marched out of that camp – yes, I say marched, for we were all such proud men and we were determined to show our captors that they had not broken us. When we got to the train – well not so much a train, but a lorry that the Japanese had converted to run on rails, to use as a train – we climbed into the trucks and started moving off. I didn't mind the conditions, for anything was better than where we had been for the last year. Out of the 1650 of us that had made that nightmare march of a year ago, there were now only just over 100 of us left alive able to be moved. We had left over 200 very sick men back at Sonkari because they were just not up to being moved. I would like to think that some of them were able to re-cover and get away from that hell hole".

"Over the next weeks we were taken to Kanburi to recuperate. Here, I was able to cook some better dishes for those very sick amongst us. I can remember the look on their faces as I tried to get them to take some food, for many of them were in such a bad way the last thing they cared about now was food, but I sat with many of them trying to get them to sip just a little of it. Thank god some of them were to recover and to this day many of them embarrass me when we are together by telling peo-ple 'this is the man that saved my life by making me eat something when I had given up'. If only they knew what they had been eating Michael, they might not say so much about it. We all had someone to thank for getting us through those days at Sonkari and I certainly had a guardian angel looking out for me at that time".

At this point I asked Stanley if he could now forgive the Japanese captors he suffered under at Sonkari. Back came his reply at once "the answer must be never, never and I will never forget". With that I gripped his hand and smiled at him for I could see he was close to tears. "Stanley I said, "I know my generation can never repay you brave men for our today, for what you had to suffer was beyond what any human should ever have to endure". He smiled back at me and said "Michael, man-kind will never learn. Look at our world today – the same thing is hap-pening these 50 years on in Bosnia etc. as it did to us all those years ago. That's the shame of it Michael, for I and my comrades believed we had suffered enough for everyone". I asked Stanley "tell me what happened to you now that you were back at Kanburi". "Well Michael, it was now the middle of 1944 and I was at last starting to feel that much better – I think just being away from Sonkari was a tonic in itself. The air you breathed was just that much better, it made you feel so much better. I began to put just a little weight back on and soon I was moved to Krangi where I cooked for the Allied Officers. I was so pleased to find that my kitchen was at the far end of the camp, well away from the Japanese. After what they had put me through, I could not bear to be near them or even hear them, such was my hatred for them at that time. I remember one poor chap coming to me to ask if I could get him a job in my kitchen. He only had one arm and looked in a sorry state. He told me 'I can't go on much more working like they make me'. I felt sorry for him and made moves to get him to work for me. This was allowed, and even though he only had one arm, he worked hard and was a valuable member of our kitchen team. He told me he had been an artist back in civvy street and had lost his arm in the sinking of the Prince of Wales. He never stopped thanking me for getting him a job in my kitchen – he would tell me every day 'you have saved my life Sergeant by getting me this job. If I can grant you any wish what would it be?' I stopped and thought to myself, what it would be that I would ask for? Then I thought.... if he is an artist he can paint me a picture of my darling Dora and this is what I asked him for. He made his own paint brushes and from paper stolen from the Japs, he produced a wonderful painting of my Dora. I had kept hidden a small photo of her that she had given me on the day we parted and this chap copied from it and created a wonderful picture for me of my beloved. I kept it well hidden out of the Japs' way and would look at it whenever I could and dream of the happy days we had spent together before the war".

"It was fast approaching Christmas 1944 now and I was very busy preparing things for the men for Christmas dinner. Many of us now believed this could be our last Christmas as prisoners and we wanted to make it as special as we could. I prepared special menus to try and bring some cheer to the men. I still can't believe the things I learnt to make out of rice but it did turn out to be a special Christmas for me. I was called up on stage after Christmas dinner and the men all cheered me. An Australian Officer presented me with a scroll that he and his fellow Officers had made and signed to thank me for my special cooking and care I had given to the sick at Krangi. As the Australian Colonel shook my hand and presented it to me, he told me that he could never thank me enough for what I had done for his men and he informed me that all his Officers had been pleased to sign it. I was so very moved by it and as I walked back to my seat one of my English Officers stopped me and asked to have a look at it. I was only too pleased to let him. He told me to destroy it. I asked 'why Sir?' He replied 'if the Japanese see it and find out what it's for, they will kill you. You were lucky to get out of it back at Sonkari when you helped the escape party but if they find this you might not be so lucky'. I said 'right Sir' but as I said it I knew it would be one order I could not follow. I went straight away and got a piece of bamboo and hollowed it out and rolled my scroll up in it along with my beloved's picture and then I buried it somewhere safe and to this day I still have them and hold them to be two of my most prized possessions".

"Soon after Christmas I met this Officer again and he said to me 'you did the right thing Sergeant, destroying that scroll'. I just replied 'yes Sir, but how did you know about my little part in the escape party from Sonkari?' He just looked at me and said 'I am in the Regiment that knows all Sergeant – 'intelligence!'. I never met him again after that but I must say he did not know everything for I was able to bring my scroll home".

"The news started to get very good now. Our secret dicky bird (as we called our hidden radio) was bringing us such very good news each day. When it brought us news that the Americans had dropped the H-bombs, after our treatment at Sonkari I wished they had dropped 22 of them on Japan. We soon heard that the war was over but we were told to keep quiet. It seemed that after several days of waiting and wondering what was to happen to us, at last we were called to parade in front of the Japanese General who informed us the war was over and we were now to be free. I can still remember the tears of joy I cried that day, I was to be one of the lucky ones, my dream of life had come true".

"A few days after the good news that the war was over, we saw allied planes coming over dropping supplies for us. One precious thing they did drop that I was glad to have was a pair of boots as mine had fallen apart on that death march to Sonkari. These were the first thing I had to put on my feet since that time and it felt quite strange wearing something on your feet again after going barefoot for so long. As well as the supplies landing we had a Lieutenant Colonel and three other ranks parachuted into Singapore that day and a few days later a company of Colonel Wingates Gurkhas marched into our camp and at last gave us protection from our little Japanese friends".

"Many of these Gurkhas lived under my hut and every morning

about four of them would escort me through the rubber plantation to my kitchen – it was always dark and so I was very glad of their escort. One morning I rushed my boots on and set off with them. I had not gone far and found my feet were hurting very badly, I thought to myself – oh no, my feet have swollen up again and ulcerated on me. The Gurkhas said 'keep up Sergeant Chown' so I struggled on until we made the kitchen. Once inside, I sat down to see what was causing me so much pain only to find that in my haste I had put my boots on the wrong feet! This made my Gurkha friends laugh and we sat and laughed so much it hurt my sides but oh how good it was to laugh again. It will be one of my better memories of those first days after the war had ended. I soon cooked us all a good breakfast and we would sit and chat about what the war had been like for us, some of the stories they told me soon let me know that the Japs did not like having to meet the Gurkhas in action". At this point I told Stanley of how my father had told me that a Gurkha only drew his knife if he was going to use it and if not he would cut himself so as to draw blood every time he took his knife out. Stanley smiled at me and said "doesn't that show you, Michael, just how dedicated the Gurkhas are? Thank God they were on our side – they are such wonderful people".

"The next few weeks were to be some of the most enjoyable that I was to spend in Singapore. I visited friends that had been lucky like me and had survived the nightmare. I saw some of the first to return from up in the jungle camps – men I had not seen since the fall of Singapore although they were in such an emaciated state that I could not even recognise them. As I looked at them it brought home to me just how bad I must have looked when I left Sonkari. I knew I had to do all I could to help these sick men and so I cooked them some light wholesome meals packed with vitamins. As I sat with many of these sick men trying to get them to eat just a little, I knew how lucky we had been that the Americans had dropped the H-bombs for I could see that none of us could have gone on for much longer and although I now know what a terrible bomb it was, I know it saved the lives of those of us that were left. I remember writing letters for those men too sick to write home and it made me feel so good to be the one to let their loved ones know that they were all right. I knew in my heart that it would most likely be the first word they had heard of them since they were captured – we just did not know for sure if the odd card that the Japanese had allowed us to fill in had really ever been sent to our families. I felt that I was doing something really good at last. To see the smiles on these poor lads' faces as they told me what to write for them was a tonic in itself, and many a time I would sit and cry tears of joy with them as they recalled happy times they had spent with their loved ones before the war. I reassured them by telling them it would not be long now before we were all back in dear old Blighty with our loved ones. I knew that would be the best medicine they, and I, could ever get. I told them it was the thought of my loved ones that had helped me get through and most of them agreed that it had been the same for them. Some said they had to survive to let the world know what the Japanese had done to them".

"I feel by sharing my story with you Michael, even though it may be 50 years too late, that long after I am dead and gone, your written word of my life will live on for other generations to know of what really happened to me and my comrades. It is to honour their memory that I am pleased to share my story with you, for as I promised that day I marched out of Sonkari, I will remember them. My hope now is that people will read and learn that war is not the answer and that only good can overcome evil. My prayer is that these things will never be allowed to happen again".

"Stanley" I asked, "when did you leave Singapore?" After he had composed himself back came his reply – "It was on the 18th September 1945 that I departed. I boarded the ship SS New Holland which was to be home to me for the next month. As we set sail that day, over the loudspeakers came the Captain's voice. He told us 'gentlemen, I am in a hurry to get home as I am sure you all are, for like you, I have not seen my loved ones for over four years.' He told us about his poor wife who had been caught up in Holland for the last four years so we knew he was speaking from the heart. One could sense the worry in his voice. After a while we came to the heavily-mined Sumatra Straits. The Captain informed us that he should really wait for an escort but, like him, we wanted to get home and so he took the decision to go it alone. We all kept lookout as well as the crew members that were posted on lookout duty. I can tell you it was heart-in-your-mouth stuff. Every time I now see a film about ships going through a minefield, I still get that cold shiver down my spine as I remember how close we came to some of them but thank God we got through and soon made full speed on to Ceylon. On arrival here we were given a great reception. All the ships that were already in harbour sounded their horns and people were cheering us. It was a great feeling to know that people appreciated what we had done for them. I think also by now some of them knew of what we had suffered under the Japanese as they could see we were all still so very thin. The first thing we were given on arrival was a haircut and a type of uniform to wear which was kind of them, for most of us only had a pair of shorts. The only trouble was this uniform was coloured jungle green and made us stand out like sore thumbs, but it was nice to have something brand new to wear after three and a half years of nothing but a Jap happy.... we felt like kings".

"Once we departed from Ceylon we moved on to the Suez Canal and on to Gibraltar and Malta where we still enjoyed the hot sun, something we had all become so used to over the last four years. As we left those climes behind us, it started to get colder, a thing we all felt so much, and most of us had to wear our greatcoats to keep warm. Then came the day we had all dreamed of over those last four years – yes, to see dear old Blighty again. We cried tears of joy that day, I can tell you. And I think it fair to say we all stood and gave a prayer of thanks as we thought of our comrades that had not been so lucky as we steamed into Liverpool. It was 16th October, four years to the day that we had left England. Our emotions were running high that day for it was a day that we had hardly dare think of over that four years away. Believe me Michael, there is no place like dear old England – she was worth fighting for. As we docked and departed the ship it was so good to see smiling faces waiting to meet their loved ones".

"Some of the men were to meet children that they never even knew about as their wives had not dare tell them that they were pregnant when they had sailed off to war those four years earlier. It was a smashing sight to see. Emotions were running so high that day that grown men were crying as much as the wives and babies, it was a sight I shall never forget".

"I spent one night in Liverpool then the next day I was made Sergeant in charge of a party of men who lived in Cambridgeshire. We were given our train passes for home and told to depart. We said our goodbyes to our dear friends waiting to depart for their own home towns and promised one another to keep in touch. As our train pulled out I discovered that the Officer that had put me in charge of my party of men had given us tickets to travel via Bletchley, putting many more hours on our journey and it was 11.00pm that night when we arrived at Cambridge station".

"It was the most important day of my life.... for there in the station mist on such a cold night stood my darling Dora. My heart was pounding so hard in my chest, but this time it was not with fear of some Jap guard – it was overflowing with my love for my beloved Dora. As I held her in my arms again it was worth all the heartache I had been through over those last few years. I think she must have thought I would squeeze all the breath out of her because I embraced her so tightly but this had been the moment I had dreamed of over those last four years – the one thing that had kept me going. We both cried tears of relief as well as the joy of being together again. We had so much to tell one another that I don't think either of us knew where to begin but over the last 50 years she has been my strength, she has always been there for me and it is only thanks to her love and care that I am here today at 84 years old. We both thank God that we have had such a wonderful life together".

"That night, as we left Cambridge station, I think it fair to say I can't remember much of the other lads meeting their loved ones for once I saw Dora that was it for me, I only had eyes for her. She got me to a taxi and we made our way to my home at Blinco Grove where my dear parents were waiting for us. The house was gaily decorated with banners of welcome home Stanley and as I embraced my dear parents I could feel the relief in their hearts to know that I was back with them again, safe, if not 100% fit. We sat and spoke of those last few years but I knew I could not let them know of what it had really been like for me. I think over the next few years they were to find out more from other people about what we had suffered for many a time I would be out with them and Dora in the town and some chap would come up to us and say 'is it really you Sergeant Chown?' My mother would say 'yes, this is him' to which the chap would reply 'oh, Sergeant Chown saved my life in Sonkari when he cooked me something really special and sat with me for days trying to get me to eat. I would not be here if it was not for him you know'. It was then that my parents would want to know more as well as my Dora and so I have been one who has spoken about it and I think it has helped me in doing so".

"The army had given me six months leave and I remember we took two wonderful holidays at Bournemouth. I spent time doing my parents gardening and I would wear the jungle green uniform that I had been given when we arrived at Ceylon. I blended in so well with the greenery that sometimes if my parents came down the garden they did not even know that I was there unless I spoke to them which would make them jump but until my parents died it was something we often had a laugh about and to this day that is really my memory of that uniform".

"After a few months of being home I wanted to be doing something so I went back to my dear old Pembroke College. They knew I had served my seven years training with them and took me on as second chef. I was just so happy to be back for it had been my dream kitchen for the last four years. In every jungle hut kitchen I had worked in over those years I always thought 'oh, if only I could be back in my Pembroke kitchen' and now here I was.... another dream had come true for me".

In 1947 my greatest wish came true for me – I married my darling Dora. A day I had dreamed about ever since I first set eyes on her. I must admit many times as a prisoner I thought it would be a day I would never see. I could not help but think on that day of all those good men that I had left back in some jungle grave. For they were never to have a day like this and something inside me was telling me just how happy they would be for me and I felt their presence with me on that wonderful day. For me it was like starting out on a new life. I tried hard to put all those nightmare days behind me now, and this is what I did until one day at College a chap said to me 'did you know a Captain David Brown who was a prisoner of the Japs and had been one of our students at Pembroke?' A cold chill came over me as I sat down, the chap said to me 'are you all right Stan?' I said 'yes, it's just come to me who this David Brown you asked me about was. Would he have been the chap who was champion bread flicker in hall?' (this was something the students seemed to do in the 1920's and 30's to see who could flick bread the furthest in the main hall at dinner). The chap replied 'yes, that's the one'. I said 'sit down a minute and I will tell you a bit about the young man', for I now remembered where I had last seen him – it was back in Singapore soon after the end of the fighting. I sat one day in the hospital trying to get some poor chap to eat something when they brought this young Officer in. He had one arm missing and his poor face was in a terrible state. I think he had caught a mortar bomb blast full on. I heard stories after this that he had dived in front of his men to protect them from the blast – he really was a very brave Officer indeed. He lost his arm and one eye and suffered terrible damage to most of his body. I knew his name of course but I could not recognise him and never imagined it could have been the young student from Pembroke. The chap said 'oh Stan, I didn't mean to upset you old mate, it's just that I knew he was one of our old students who had been a prisoner like you'. I replied 'that's all right. The College can be very proud of him for he was one of the bravest young men I have ever met and I met some very brave men in my time at Sonkari'. After things like this it would stay with me for a few days as my memories of those times always came flooding back and the nightmares would start up again but through it all I knew how lucky I was for I had come home and Dora and I were having such a wonderful life together. I was to meet this brave man, Captain Brown, when he brought his son to start College life but I found like most brave men, he did not want to talk about those nightmare times for him. Perhaps it was because he had his son with him but I did not mind for I knew already what he had been through. He did remember that I had given him the very last card I had received from Dora, one showing the Wren Chapel. Although it was very precious to me, I felt at that time he was suffering so much that it would be something to remind him of home and help give him strength to come through his pain. I like to think it did help him".

"As you know Michael, I spent the rest of my working life at Pembroke College. 50 years service I gave them, and yes I just wish I could do it all again – such happy times, even if it was hard work. I became Head Chef and then I became Chef Manager. I worked hard and many times when I was preparing a banquet I lost all track of time and many times Dora would come to find me and say to me 'do you know it's nearly midnight?' I would reply 'no I didn't darling, it can't be that late already'. 'Well it is' she would say, 'and you are coming home now'. That's how much I loved my work Michael, I never even knew what the time was, once I was absorbed in my work. My dear Dora must have thought at times I loved my work more than her but I can assure you I love her more than life itself, she is everything to me".

"During my working life I met many wonderful people and I cooked for many VIP's from royalty to politicians. I was awarded as a fellow of the Catering and Food Association and a Master Craftsman of the Guild of Chefs, plus many awards and certificates for my cooking and cake confectionery designs. Of all the people I cooked for I was always pleased to cook for the late Canon Duckworth and I became a good friend of his and I am pleased to say spent many happy occasions with him. He was a true hero to the world. If ever a man was God on earth doing nothing but good for mankind, it was Canon Duckworth".

"I remember cooking for Prince Charles when he would eat at our College even though he was up at Trinity studying, and a thing I shall never forget is that proud day when he presented me with the MBE at Buckingham Palace. I was so pleased that as he presented me with my medal he remembered me and made time to chat to me about his happy times at College. When I think of the people he meets it pleased me so much to think he remembered a small everyday person like me".

"Towards the later part of my career at Pembroke, not long before I retired, the Bursar came to see me one day to tell me a Japanese conference was coming to the College. He handed me a list of the dates that they were to be at College. I told him that 'with respect, Sir, I would take that whole month off for I can't say how I will react, and I certainly would not want to let the College down'. I told him 'when you have seen your best friends kicked to death by them and have suffered unbelievable things at their hands I think it only fair to say I don't like them,

Sir'. I thought no more about it, as I now knew the dates they would be at College and knew I would not be about, but one day out of the blue as I was working I heard Japanese voices. Even after all these years it brought a chill right through my body. I took some deep breaths and calmed myself. I walked up to them and in Japanese I asked 'can I help you?'. They looked knocked back to hear an English Chef talking to them in their own language. They told me they were the three Japanese men that had come to arrange their conference. Amongst much bowing from them, which I quite enjoyed, they handed me a list of names of their people that would be attending. As I took a quick look through it I saw the name Wokerryarsher – the name of the barbaric Japanese Officer in charge at Sonkari. I told the conference organiser that when they all arrived I would like to meet this one man. I did not tell them why but I knew then that I would not take the month off for this was one man I wanted to see. Could it possibly be him? What would I do to him if it was? My mind was racing with revenge and once again I found all those nightmare memories coming back to haunt me. I remembered the Jap guard who had told me 'you all go Singapore soon' and I remembered the Jap guard who was so afraid that he had cholera that he took himself off and shot himself. And yes, I thought of my dear friends that had not come home and of those that had come home but had just been like living dead. Was I now to be the one to revenge them? I put myself into my work to keep my mind off the subject for I knew I would give them a banquet to be proud of, for my College had to come first and whatever my outcome with Wokerryarsher I knew that the Japanese had to see how well we lived".

"The day they were to arrive soon came and the first thing I knew of them being there was while I was laying out the main table. This little Jap chap came running up to me and in his broken English ranted on 'Mr Chown, Mr Chown. I Wokerryarsher. My father was jeweller. He no in war'. I looked at him and laughed and said 'don't worry. I am pleased to meet you'. But obviously those three conference organisers had told him about me and he must have known something about the barbaric Wokerryarsher to come to me in such a worried state, but I could see he was only young and to this day probably does not know what his people put us through".

"I did my best to make their conference a happy one and I could see they were a world apart from those Japanese that had caused me so much pain and suffering. They really were so kind to me and showered me with gifts and even brought gifts for my dear Dora. They all wanted photos of me decorating salmons for they had enjoyed eating them so much they wanted to show their families back home just how good they had looked before they had devoured them. It certainly showed me that there were some charming Japanese, far different from the ones I had seen all those years before. I still can't forgive or forget but I do know that there is good and bad in every country and we must all pray that good will always overcome evil".

"I have enjoyed sharing my story with you Michael, and if it helps those still suffering from tropical illness and mental war trauma, then it's even more worthwhile. Please keep up your good work and all power to your pen".

Thank you so much Stanley for sharing your story with me and for allowing me to share it with my readers. We all owe you and your comrades so very much and so it is with such pride that I thank you on behalf of all of us that have been spared the horrors of war. Thanks to all you brave men.

I could not finish Stanley's story without telling you of the sickness he suffered in his years of captivity:

- The loss of half his body weight
- Dengee Fever
- Cardiac Beri-Beri
- Malaria 33 times (still suffers some sort of relapse)
- Malnutrition and Privation associated with nervous features (suffered two nervous breakdowns)
- Lumbar Spondylosis
- Strongylordiasis (tropical worms in blood) - The thing that took my own father
- Duodenal Ulcers (has two large scars to prove it)
- Bilateral Sensorpeural (hearing loss)

I mention the scars on the outside shown from his ulcer operations but what of the scars that Stanley and his comrades have carried on the inside all these years. At the time of writing Stanley has just celebrated his 84th birthday. I pray that God will grant him and his dear Dora many more happy years together for our world will miss the likes of such great people.

Thank you Stanley.

"F" FORCE IN THAILAND, APRIL - DECEMBER 1943

*In April, 1943, Major-General Arimura, G.O.C. Allied Prisoners-of-War in
Malaya, issued orders that "F" Force, to be composed of 3,600 Australians and
3,400 British, should proceed by rail from Changi Camp, Singapore, to a northern destination. These orders further stated that 30% of the 7,000 were to be
unfit men. In answer to enquiries, Major-General Arimura's Headquarters
explained that the journey would entail no marching, and that the force was not
required for labour but was destined for 'health camps' in a good climate, where
food would be abundant and the unfit would have a better chance of recovery
than at Changi. These orders, and the shortage of fit personnel at Changi,
caused the inclusion in the force of 2,000 unfit men, while the majority of the
remaining 5,000 also had had some kind of medical history since the capitulation, many of them being recent convalescents from such diseases as diphtheria,
dysentery and beri-beri. All were reduced in strength already by malnutrition
during the previous year: and the promise of better food and treatment put
everyone in high spirits at departure.*

*The Force entrained at Singapore during the latter part of April, 1943, in
13 separate parties at one-day intervals and proceeded, crowded into steel rice-
trucks, 27 men to a truck, to Bampong in Thailand. The train journey lasted 4
to 5 days. Food and water were scarce throughout and none were available
during the last 24 hours of the journey.*

*As each party arrived at Bampong it learned that the Force was faced with
a march of indefinite length as no transport was available. Consequently, all
the heavy equipment of the Force, including hospital equipment, medical supplies, tools and cooking gear and all personal kit which could not be carried on
the man, had to be abandoned in an unguarded dump at Bampong. Practically
the whole of this material (including three-quarters of the medical stores) was
lost to the Force throughout the 8 months spent up-country, as the immediate
advent of the monsoon (at the usual season) prevented the Japanese from moving more than a negligible proportion of it by lorry.*

*The march of 300 kilometres which followed would have been arduous for
fit troops in normal times. For this Force, burdened with its sick and short of
food, it proved a trial of unparalleled severity. The road had a loose metal
surface for the first two stages but then degenerated into an old elephant track,
widened into a hazardous dry-weather trail, through dense and mountainous
jungle. The march was carried out in stages of 20 to 30 kilometres and lasted
2½ weeks. The parties always marched at night: the monsoon broke in earnest
soon after the march began and conditions rapidly worsened. Everyone was
loaded to capacity and such medical equipment of the Force as could be carried
was distributed to individuals. Men toiled through the pitch blackness and tor-*

rential rain, sometimes knee-deep in water, sometimes staggering off bridges in the dark; sprains and bruises were common, fractures of arms and legs occurred and stragglers were set upon and looted by marauding Thais. Of the large and growing number of sick, many fell by the wayside and they and their kit had to be carried by their comrades.

At the staging-camps, Which were merely roadside clearings in the jungle, there was no overhead cover: it was sometimes a long carry for water and it was impossible for men to rest properly. Food generally consisted of rice and onion stew with hot water to drink and often of rice only. This was insufficient to maintain health and entirely inadequate to support the physical strain of a march of this description. These staging-camps were in charge of truculent Japanese N.C.O.s, who demanded large fatigue-parties when the men should have been resting and forcibly drove the sick onto the road with blows to continue the march night after night, in spite of the protests of their officers.

On arrival at the destination (five jungle-camps spread over a distance of 50 kilometres in close proximity to the Thailand-Burma border) it was found that the camps had not been completed and all ranks were housed in unroofed huts, exposed to the continual downpour of the monsoon rains, which continued without intermission for the next five months. From most of these camps men were taken out to work by the Japanese engineers as soon as they arrived, without opportunity to rest, although many of them had just completed six successive nightmarches and were in the last stages of exhaustion.

Unlike all other P.O.Ws in Thailand, "F" Force remained nominally under the administration of Major-General Arimura's headquarters at Changi, Singapore. The local Japanese commander was Lt. Col. Banno, who proved incapable either of administering the Force or of protecting its personnel from the outrageous demands and treatment of the Japanese engineers, under whom it was put to work. The camps were commanded by junior Japanese Officers or N.C.O.s of the Malaya P.O.W. Administration and the guards were Koreans. The former, with one exception, were entirely subservient to the engineers, or themselves actively hostile, while some of the Koreans also treated the prisoners with senseless cruelty. The Officers and men of the engineers, whose sole responsibility to the prisoners was to make them work, behaved with calculated and extreme brutality from start to finish.

Cholera broke out in the first camp early in May. This was directly attributable to the criminal negligence of the Japanese. For at Konkoita, the last staging-camp but two, every one of the fifteen marching-parties was forced to camp for one or more days within a few yards of huts filled with hundreds of cholera-stricken coolies, on ground covered with infected faeces, where the air was black with flies. British officers asked for the loan of spades to remove this filth, but the Japanese replied contemptuously, "use your hands". Lt. Col. Harris protested *vigorously to Lt. Col. Banno, warning him of the inevitable consequences and demanding that either all forward movement should be stopped or that the infection-point should be by-passed. But nothing was done. The march forward continued and by the end of May cholera was epidemic in all five labour-camps.*

The work demanded of all men, without consideration of their physical condition, was heavy navvy-labour on the rushed construction of a 50 kilometre stretch of the Burma-Thailand railway, through hilly and flooded jungle, immediately south of the Three Pagodas Pass. This work was arduous in the extreme, men having to carry logs far beyond their strength and pile-drive up to their waists in water. The hours were generally from first light to dark, but frequently men were kept out as late as 2 a.m. the following morning. Men working in quarries without boots had their feet badly cut and these cuts developed into tropical ulcers. Through incessant work in deep mud, trench feet became practically universal and rapidly developed into ulcers also.

There were daily beatings of officers and men at work, sometimes even into unconsciousness. These beatings were not disciplinary purposes but were intended to urge sick and enfeebled men to physical efforts quite beyond their remaining strength, or to punish Officers for intervening on their behalf.

Every morning the same grim spectacle was repeated in the various camps of parading men for work at first light. Emerging from their crowded huts or leaky shelters in the pouring rain, even the fitter men appeared gaunt and starving, clad in rags or merely loincloths, most of them bootless and with cut and swollen feet. In addition, some 50 or 60 sick men from "hospital", leaning on sticks or squatting in the mud would be paraded to complete the quota and would become the subject of a desperate argument between their Officers and the Japanese engineers. Sometimes all of these, sometimes only a part, would be taken out to work and would leave the camp hobbling on sticks or half-carried by their comrades.

Many of the fitter men had not seen their camp in daylight for many weeks and had had no opportunity of washing themselves or their clothes.

The P.O.W.s Headquarters, under Lt. Col. S.W. Harris, OBE RA was handicapped by the obstinacy of the Japanese in refusing access to the various camps and by Lt. Col. Banno's failure to make protests felt by the engineers or ameliorate conditions himself as required. Written protests and appeals to Major-General Arimura were never answered. Only once was direct access to the Regimental Commander of the Engineers obtained and that by chance, when a personal appeal by Lt. Col. Harris and his staff resulted in the postponement of an order which would have caused the immediate and permanent expulsion of 700 desperately sick and dying men from their hospital hut into open jungle during the worst of the monsoon rains, to make way for a native labour-force. This order had already been endorsed by Lt. Col. Banno's administration.

Mike Bentinck promoting "Forgotten Heroes" at Burrows Bookshop in Ely

George Street (FEPOW) and Mike Bentinck in Burrows Bookshop.

Mike Bentinck and Stan Chown with Mayoress of Cambridge at a dinner given for surviving Cambridgeshire FEPOW's and Burma Star Veterans

Canon Duckworth (left) at a reunion dinner.

A message of 'Thanks' to the Americans from Percy (front row right) and fellow prisoners.

1995 FEPOW Dinner in Sawston. Photo: Cambridgeshire Newspapers Ltd.

FEPOW VJ Day 50th Anniversary Party. Photo: Cambridgeshire Newspapers Ltd.

Mike Bentinck with Gill Manley, radio presenter for BBC Hereford and Worcester.

Mike "On Air" during one his many radio broadcasts around the country.

Percy Legge.

Percy Legge as a prisoner.

Percy Legge and Sgt. Ager in Canada.

Some of the Japanese suffered too.

Stan Chown and Dora on their wedding day in 1947.

Stan and Dora in 1995.

Stan with some of his many culinary masterpieces prepared whilst at Pembroke College, Cambridge.

The Wren Chapel at Pembroke College created in icing by Stan.

Sgt. Ager (centre) with the rice box they used for their rations whilst prisoners.

Mike Bentick and his mother at a the FEPOW memorial in Milton, Cambridgeshire.

The hospital, so called, in every camp was nothing but a dilapidated hut with leaky roof, no walls or lighting and with split-bamboo flooring on which the men were crammed, their bodies touching one another. In these grossly over-crowded conditions even such few mosquito nets as the Japanese provided could not be used, with the result that over 90% of the Force were speedily infected with malaria. Sleeping mats and blankets were never made available except in negligible quantities.

The attitude of the Japanese towards the sick was a mixture of callous indifference and active spite: for by their sickness they were regarded as imped-ing the Japanese war effort. Two remarks made, at official interviews, by Lieut. Fukuda, commander of one of the camps, will serve to illustrate this attitude:-"International Law and the Geneva Convention do not apply if they conflict with the interests of the Japanese Army"; and again (to a senior Australian Medical Officer), "You have in the past spoken somewhat boastfully of the Ge-neva Convention and humanity. You must remember that you are our prisoners of war, that you are in our power and that under present circumstances these things do not apply".

Although cholera killed approximately 750 of the Force, by far the most deadly disease was dysentery, aggravated by malnutrition and generally com-plicated by malaria or beri-beri or both. Over a long period no food was avail-able for such patients except rice and beans and the quantities provided for the sick were deliberately reduced by the Japanese to starvation point in the express belief that this would compel them to go out to work. The inevitable result was that hundreds of men died in a condition of extreme emaciation and complete despair.

By the 20th June, two months after leaving Changi, only 700 men of the Force were out at work and most of these were sick, while the remainder, except for the small administrative and medical parties, were lying in improvised 'hos-pitals' in each of the labour-camps.

By the end of July the position of the Force was desperate. Communication between the camps and either Burma or Thailand was ceased owing to impass-able roads and broken bridges: 1800 of the Force had died. In one camp alone the following diseases were prevalent:- cholera, typhus, spinal meningitis, small-pox, diphtheria, jaundice, pneumonia, pleurisy, malaria, dysentery, scabies, beri-beri and tropical ulcers. With the exception of quinine, there were very few drugs and no dressings available throughout the whole area and hideous tropi-cal ulcers were dressed with banana leaves and puttees, or with dressings impro-vised from old shorts or shirts. The result was that some 70 amputations of limbs were necessary, entirely due to lack of dressings and because the men suffering from ulcers had been forced out to work by the Japanese. Deaths in one camp alone (Sonkurai) were then averaging 12 a day and of the original 1,600

65

British troops who marched into that camp in May, 1,200 were dead before December.

By the end of December, when the Force arrived back in Singapore, more than 3,000 men were dead out of the original 7,000 who had set out in April and 1,000 had been left behind in Burma or Thailand either as sick incapable of surviving the journey, or as medical and administrative personnel in charge of them. Of the 3,000 survivors who returned to Singapore, 95% were heavily infected with malaria, 80% were suffering from general debility and 50% required hospital treatment for a long period, chiefly through dysentery, beri-beri, chronic malaria, skin-disease and malnutrition. Six weeks after their return two Japanese Medical Officers examined these 3,000 survivors, with a view to selecting men for further work on aerodrome construction. They could find 125, fit for light duty, only.

The events narrated here took place, not in the comparative security of a permanent P.O.W. Camp but in the remoteness of the Thailand jungle and at the hands of a callous and vindictive enemy; they persisted over a long period, to which at the time no end could be foreseen except the likelihood of death by starvation, ill-treatment and disease. Here was no heat and excitement of war and yet the hardships and privations endured by all were as bad as any likely to be met with on active service and the casualties were unfortunately at least as great.

In these conditions, the unbroken spirit of the Force and the steady devotion to duty of many Officers, N.C.O.s and men, themselves often seriously ill, were indeed remarkable.

CHAPTER THREE

Percival Legge's Story

Friends, I share with you now another true story from another of my heroes – a man I am so privileged to be able to call my friend. As you will see, he is another who has given and suffered so much for our today. I am just so pleased that he has chosen me to record his story for others to read how he and his comrades have marked the paths of history and, like me, his hopes and prayers are that such pain and suffering will never be allowed to happen again. It is my privilege now to share with you Percy's story.

Percy was born at Southery, a village not far from Ely, Cambridge-shire – a fen village. He grew up in typical village life where everyone knew everybody's business but cared about one another and would do all they could to help one another, for that was village life. In the 1920s and 30s no one needed to lock their doors. It was a time when everyone felt safe and life was good, for even in the fens with the effects of recession around the country, people had to eat and so the people of the fens were kept busy producing food. Farming was big business at that time and there was work for the men of the village. Percy's father had served in the Cambridgeshire Regiment in the first world war, was wounded in action in France and had been sent home to recover from his wounds. As he recovered from his wounds he met his wife to be at Felixstowe, where she was working on the trams – just two ordinary people who fell in love and married. He brought his wife home to the fens and started married life. He thought, like everyone, that he had seen the last of war, as the war to end all wars had now been fought and he had his scars to prove the part he had played in it. Young Percy attended Southery school and played the games most boys do – yes, playing soldiers and of course cowboys and indians.... they were happy days. Percy had a great love of horses and was always looking for the chance to work the land with them, and to care for them (and earn a bob or two) by helping on the local farms. Percy learnt to look after himself, if the need arose. He would find his fenland upbringing to stand him in good stead for he had learnt to set traps and snares etc. and of course, shooting. He excelled at sport and by the time he was a teenager he had grown to a strapping six-footer and had the perfect physique to match his height, the one thing that would go against him in the years to come. But the lessons he learned on the land were to stand him in good stead.

Not long after Percy had left school and started work on the farms, his father took a pub, the Anchor Inn at Little Ouse. It was now 1937 and Percy was enjoying life to the full. He loved his job and had over 40 horses to work and care for on the farm where he worked. His boss could see he had a natural way with horses and Percy told me they had always been part of his life. His grandfather had run a farm and also had horses and Percy had been brought up with them, so to speak.

When his work was finished for the day, he always had a good night life for living in a pub was to offer plenty to do on cold winter nights such as darts, dominoes, crib etc. besides good beer to drink. He had plenty of good mates and always had lots to do – in his own words he was such a lucky chap.

In 1939 on May 10th, Percy and seven of his mates went up town to Littleport for a night out as it was the day before Percy's 19th birthday. As they passed the town hall they could see a sign up saying 'join the territorial army'. Percy had often thought of joining the army but was worried what his father would say. He and his mates stood looking at the notice board and one of the lads said "come on mates let's go in and join up. They say it's good fun you know; they go to camp and have weekends away you know. Come on, let's do it". Percy and the others said "OK let's go in, it won't hurt just to enquire will it". As they stepped inside Percy found himself pushed to the front and a Recruiting Officer called Lieutenant Cutlack stepped up to him and said "that's it young man, walk this way and sign here. I can see you will make a fine young soldier. You are a strapping lad". As Percy followed Lieutenant Cutlack to the desk and started to talk to him, he noticed that his mates had gone but as Percy spoke to Lieutenant Cutlack something was telling Percy that this would be a good thing to do and so he signed up. All he was worried about now was what his father would say about it.

When he got outside and found his mates who were laughing at how they had left him to it. They said "Percy, you ain't joined have you?" Percy looked at them with such pride and said "yes I have". Some of the others said "you bloody fool. We were only messing about. We didn't mean you to join up. You know if there's a war again you will be one of the first to be called up now you know". Percy looked at them and re-plied "I don't mind that, if it means helping my country. It's the least I can do, for my dad did his bit in the last war and anyway you know that was the war to end all wars so there's no worry of that is there". "Come on" shouted one of his mates, "we shall have all the pubs closed before we even get a drink at this rate, let's go on with enjoying ourselves". So off they went for their night on the town.

As Percy drove home that night he was thinking again about what his father would say about it and as he drew into the pub yard it was now quite late. He walked in the back door and was met by his father who was busy changing the barrels and tidying up. "Hello there son" said his father, "had a good night out?" Percy replied "yes dad but I have got something I must tell you" to which his dad replied "well don't look so worried, let's get a night cap and sit down and then you can tell me all about it. Now you sit down here son while I get us that drink". Percy sat down, his hands were sweating, his heart was racing, for he felt so worried at what his father would think about it all for he could well remember his fathers stories of war and knew how badly he had been wounded and it was these things that were causing Percy so much anguish in his mind – he had such respect for his father that he would do nothing to cause him any upset. While Percy sat with these thoughts running through his mind, his father returned to the table and passed Percy his night cap and sat down with him. "Right son, let's have it then, what's worrying yea then?" Percy took a deep breath and in one big rush out it all came "dad I've joined the Terris". His dad looked at him and with a smile on his face said "good for you lad". Percy said "don't you mind then, dad? Its been worrying me all night what you would say about it".

"Son I'm proud of you" his father replied, "it's up to you, son, what you do. You're a man now and must follow your own heart you know what's right and wrong and if you follow your heart and always try to do the right thing by others you won't go far wrong old son. Now let's get these drinks down us and get to bed". As Percy downed his drink he stood up and smiling at his dad, he said "look at the time, it's gone midnight". His father replied "yes it is son, so happy birthday and goodnight". Percy said "thanks so much dad, goodnight" and made his way upstairs to bed. He fell asleep that night a happy man for he now knew his dad did not mind. The next morning as he came down he was met by his mother and sister who greeted him with birthday wishes and presents. He told them what he had done and was pleased at their reaction. His sister told him "you'll have all the girls after you in uniform you know". His father entered the room and said "you won't mind that one bit will you Percy lad?" to which Percy replied "no dad, I think I can stand that". Percy had already met the girl for him in his words. She was so good looking, so caring and everything any man could ever want. Her name was Joyce and Percy knew then that she was to be the only girl for him.

Over the next few months Percy enjoyed his time with the Territorial Army. He told me how on the first night after joining up he reported to the drill hall at Ely where he found about another 200 chaps that had joined so he soon made many new friends. In August 1939 they all went to Dibgate camp where they all slept in tents, there were no beds, just three wooden boards given to each man to lay on. Percy was to find that from now on his days of sleeping in feather beds were numbered. He was woken at 6.00am by Reveille and got in line for his cup of tea and biscuit then it was a five mile cross country run followed by more training and drilling etc. At night they would go for long walks and then back to the camp fire for a sing-song before turning in for the night. Such happy times, lots of good mates and above all, a feeling of doing something worthwhile. The thing Percy remembered most about this camp was the rumours of war. Many of the chaps were saying "they won't let us home now you know, they will keep us all together now as a unit ready for the off'. But this was not to be and Percy and the others did get home. However, a day or two later Percy was working on the farm at Little Ouse when his boss a Mr Morton came up to him and said "Percy my old son, you have got to report to the drill hall at Ely by tomorrow as things are not too good, as you know". Percy replied "I shall finish my days work Mr Morton and report at the drill hall tomorrow morning if that's all right with you, sir". Mr Morton took hold of Percy's hand and gripped it tightly and said "don't worry old son, you and your mates will soon have those so and so's sorted out and you will be back here with us in no time at all". Percy finished his days work and said his goodbyes to his work mates for he knew in his heart this was it – this was to be the real thing now, no more playing at part time soldiers for war had raised its ugly head again and, as they say, 'England expects every man to do his duty'.

Percy could not sleep that night with all that was running through his mind, so it was an early start for him that Saturday. His mother cooked him a good breakfast and as he left the Anchor Inn that day his father embraced him and told him "remember what I told you that night son – follow your heart and do what's right by others and you will be fine". Percy drove off to Ely that morning with very mixed feelings. His emotions were very high but as soon as he arrived at the drill hall and met up with all the others he was fine. After all the formalities were over, Percy was told to go home and collect his belongings and then report to a Mrs Tucker's house in Ely. As he drove back home everything was running through his mind – on one hand he was excited on the other he was worried, not so much for himself, but for his loved ones, for he knew it was to be goodbye to those he loved most in his life. His thoughts went to his dear girlfriend Joyce, who he had known since they were very young teenagers. He knew he loved her so much and was so worried how she would cope. As he arrived at the Anchor Inn there she was to meet him with his mother, father and sister and all the regulars at the Inn. He told them all what he had to do and he and Joyce got his things together and said their goodbyes. He also said his goodbyes to his parents and his sister and went outside where he was collected and taken to his billet at Ely. Percy had three days at Mrs Tucker's while being informed by his superiors at the Ely drill hall of what he was to do now that he was a proper soldier. On the fourth day he was sent to Wisbech and billeted at the Dukes Head pub – home from home for Percy. It was run by a Mr and Mrs Place. While here Percy was put in charge of three other chaps that had also been billeted there – Roy Hitch, C Ruttherford and a chap called Lucky Tunnel. But as Percy told me "there was no real need for anyone to be in charge, for we were all mates now and got on well together".

"At night when the pub closed we would help Mr Place tidy up then he would give us all a free pint and we would sit and chat together and have some bread and cheese – he was very good to us all at that time. In the mornings we would report to our headquarters, the Old Brewery in Wisbech, to receive our days orders. One day I was out training when a Lance Corporal Jugg came up to me and told me to report at once to HQ. This I did and was informed that I and Lance Corporal Jugg were to report to our HQ at Cambridge to attend a bren carrier course as our company were forming a carrier platoon. As Corporal Jugg and I collected our things I said to him 'but I know nothing about bren gun carriers' to which he replied 'nor do I mate, but don't worry, it's got to be better than all this drill. At least we can sit and drive the thing and save our plates of meat from getting sore' ".

"We arrived at Cambridge and were soon billeted and over the next 10 days we attended the carrier course and were shown how to maintain them, drive them and use them against the enemy if the need arose. After 10 days we were given a test on all the things we had been taught. We both passed with flying colours which pleased us and our CO. We were sent back to Wisbech which pleased me for I was very happy at Mr and Mrs Place's pub. I received my first stripe and Stan Jugg received his second and became a full Corporal. We were given our carrier and informed that nobody was to touch it but us, which suited us just fine. We were instructed that we were to teach the others in the platoon how to drive the carrier – we would take two men out in the morning and two in the afternoon with some days carrying out maintenance. Sometimes we even had to take Officers out to train them and one of these Officers was just terrible. Try as we may, we could not get him to learn how to drive it. In the end we just gave him such a rough ride each time he was only too pleased to get himself moved from the carrier platoon. We made sure we never passed anyone too soon as this was such a good number we did not want it to end. No route marches for us now, we just sat back and let the carrier do all the work".

"Over the next few months Corporal Jugg and I went all over East Anglia teaching chaps about bren gun carriers. On the 1st of November, we went to Melton Constable and were billeted at a Mr Mason's house but we found it very quiet here with nothing to do – after staying in a pub we had been spoilt! On the 1st of December we moved off again to Holt and were billeted with a family that had young children. This did not work out though, as at night when we returned to the house the carrier would wake the children up, so we were moved to an empty cottage called Yew Tree. Here we had no beds and just slept on the floor. It was very cold now and we were only given a little coal so we used to go out at nights and collect some from the railway station. The food at this time was not too good so we got hold of as much bread as we could from the mess hall, then at night we would sit around the fire and toast it and have it with some dripping on it. We were having to work hard now as it was a hard winter and we were kept busy digging out trains that had got snowed in. One day I went to collect the carrier from outside the local school but when I went to move it the tracks had frozen to the road and so I could not get it to turn – it shot forward and knocked the drain pipes clean off the school wall. I then had to report to Major Eagle and tell him what I had done. He was not very pleased and told me to 'take more care, boy, you're our expert on the thing, old son. Perhaps we'd better not use it while this bad weather is with us. I think you should get home and have some Christmas leave'. I was not going to argue with him on that and was only too pleased to get home for Christmas".

"Joyce came down to the Anchor Inn for Christmas day with us and I went to hers for Boxing Day. Looking back it was to be the best Christmas I would have for a long time. The very next day I returned to Holt, to Yew Tree cottage, and soon got the fire started again to try and keep warm. January 1940 soon came round and we were moved to Stiffky, near Wells. It was still very cold and we were billeted in huts with only wooden bed boards to sleep on again. We could not do much training because of the weather but at night if we got a pass out, we would walk to

Wells, which was a good walk from camp. Our Sergeant Long was in charge of policing and woe betide anyone caught out without a pass. He was given two weeks leave as he had worked over Christmas and New Year and I was chosen to take on his duties while he was away. I was given a little motor to drive round in and felt very chuffed at being chosen. I never did report anyone and the two weeks soon passed but it did show me the perks of being a Corporal. It was not long after this that I was asked to build a rifle range which I did in an old disused gravel pit just outside Stiffky camp on the main road to Wells for the whole battalion to use. I had to take men there and train them at shooting. After a while once everyone got used to it, I would get them to put a few pence in a kitty then we would have a weekly shoot off and the winner would have a little bit extra beer money. I had my fair share of wins and I think it made it that bit more interesting for all the chaps. I can assure you it helped raise the standard of shooting in the battalion".

"One day while at the range an Officer from my platoon, a captain Page, came to me and informed me that the battalion was to have a cross country run. He said 'you look very fit to me Corporal, I think you will make a good runner so give it your best my man'. A few days later we all set off on the cross country run. As I was running along I was thinking to myself what a good life I was having in the army and soon realised how lucky I was to be with my carrier, most of the time. I thought to myself if this Officer wants me to be a runner for the battalion then I will give it my best. I got my head down and got going; we covered about 10 miles on this run and I finished third which pleased me no end. After a couple of weeks of these runs the Officers picked out 12 of us and to my surprise I was made team captain. The Officer told me that I could take the team training at any time, all I had to do was let him know when and where we would be running. The other 11 chaps and I had a wonderful time after that – we trained hard, but it did get us away from a lot of the everyday army life and we enjoyed people calling out to us as we ran through their village. I remember one particular day we were to race against the 4th Norfolk's and our Padre Duckworth, who was also sports mad, said to me 'if your lads win today, I shall buy you all new shorts and vests and have the battalion crest put on them'. I told the other lads this and I can tell you we ran our hearts out that day.... and won. Padre Duckworth, always a man of his word, soon came up with our new kit and I was so proud to have our Cambridgeshire badge across my chest, as were the other lads. For me I had found something I was good at, a sport I had never even thought of before and it was making me so fit and bringing me so many good perks. Not long after we had won this particular race a Platoon Officer came up to me and informed me that each company had to send an NCO to attend a P.T. course and he told me 'I have put your name forward so don't let me down or else'. Officers were always nice like that you know – always ready to give you that extra need to do well!"

"I attended the course which was held at Gresham school, Holt. Many a time we had to play games which meant holding hands. We all felt like a load of nancies prancing about, at times. The chap I nearly always got to hold hands with was to turn out to be a life long best friend to me; he used to say 'bloody rough old hands to give me to hold' which they were what with working on the land and now working on the carriers. He was a Sergeant from D Company and I know you will know of him and if ever a braver man walked on this earth then I have yet to meet him – yes, it was Len Gilbey and, as I say, we were to become the best of friends right up until Len's time came to leave this world." [Many of you will remember Len Gilbey from Robert Driver's story in 'Forgotten Heroes' when Len lost his arm in the action to take out a Japanese machine gun post].

"It was very hard work on the P.T. course and I thought I was fit after all my running, but this was to find muscles that I never knew I had, but once they stopped aching it was good fun. When we passed the course we were given long blue trousers with red stripes down the sides and a jumper with red and black stripes around the body. We looked a bit like Dennis the Menace but we thought we looked very smart. We were then sent on to another course where once we passed we were awarded the cross swords badge which we had to sew on the arms of our jumpers. This brought us extra pay, not much, but it all helped towards your beer money which then was the highlight of your day to be able to relax and enjoy a pint with your mates in the evening and chat away about home life".

"May 1940 came and we were all given lots of inoculations and then the best gift of all – I was given a weeks leave. It meant so much to me to be going home to see my dear Joyce again and my family. It was a real tonic but a week soon flies by and before I knew it I was on my way back to Stiffky. On my arrival back at camp I found the battalion had moved out and I and six other chaps had to sleep in a tent, but it was now warm evenings so I did not mind".

"I was given a stretch of coast to cover which took in Salthouse where my mate Len was stationed. I don't know what the powers that be thought I could do on my own with just one bren gun carrier if the Germans did invade for I had miles to cover all on my own so thank

God they did not invade. On my way back to camp each evening I would call in at Salthouse to see Len. My mother had sent me a bottle of port for my birthday and I had kept it in the carrier, so one evening I got it out and Len and I saw it off. It was such a happy evening. I think the old carrier knew its own way back to camp by now, anyway, for I can't remember much about getting back to camp that evening".

"July 1940 soon arrived and I was moved back to Gresham School at Holt where I was given more inoculations. Also now the training was very hard with lots of guard drill and foot slogging which I was made to do as well. I also had much more training to do with the carrier and went out with many other company's carriers. Then came the news that we were to be inspected by Winston Churchill so we were all kept busy making everywhere spick and span. When the day of the inspection came, I stood right at the end of the row beside my carrier. He walked along the row and came up to where I was with the carrier, tapped the carrier with his stick and said 'we shall have to get a lot more of these Corporal', to which I replied 'yes Sir' but I must say they were a long time in coming".

"In August 1940 I was given even more inoculations and then informed that the carrier platoon was to be based at Sherringham. I was to make my way there and was told I was to stay at the Sherringham Hotel which suited me just fine – the food was excellent as was the accommodation – it really was top notch. While here I joined up with a lot of the other companies with carriers, I had some great times with the Norfolk Regiment and the people of Norfolk were so very kind to me. I had a few bad times while at Sherringham though, as quite a few bombs were dropped on us but the people of Sherringham all pulled together and looked after one another so well that I could see it would take more than a few German bombs to break their spirit. I stayed for 10 days at Aylsham in Norfolk with the Norfolk lads to teach them about carriers. They were good lads and I think we all got on well because many of them had worked on the land and we had so much in common. I was then moved on to Fakenham where I billeted in the crown yard where for the first time I kept my carrier in a garage at the back of the yard. I remember I used to get a bath here for 6d and as there were lots of young ladies working here, I think we all spent a lot on baths, but after a day on the carrier you really needed one anyway".

"Saturday was market day and the town would be packed, all the farmers would come into town and they would treat us to a drink – it was a real job to keep sober. They were so kind to us. I wonder now if they had some idea of what we would be in for – many of them had fought in the great war and still carried the scars to prove it but they were such nice people to us – I shall always remember Fakenham as being such a kind place. In September 1940, D Company was moved to Raynham Hall and I was stationed in the stables at the rear of the hall. There was one pub here called the Greyhound – we had some good nights there, I can tell you!"

"Len Gilbey was here and was Sergeant in charge of D Company's training. Sometimes on the way back to camp I would drive past them all slogging along and would shout out to Len and wave and he would shout 'it's alright for you'. I would then make him even more angry by shouting back to him 'you look a bit red in the face old mate, you try and take it a bit slower'. You can imagine what all the other blokes would shout out, but Len would shake his fist and shout 'I'll get you later you old so and so' but when we met later in the pub we always laughed it off and I would buy him a pint. Looking back they were such happy times".

"October 1940 came and we were still at Raynham Hall, but it was good here the food was good. There was also lots of game about – pheasants and rabbits – and the carrier platoon always had plenty of guns on board in the large tool box. We had a twelve bore, a 410 and even a 16 bore. We always found someone willing to buy our kills as most of the locals liked rabbit stew etc. There was always a rumour at Raynham Hall that it was haunted by a ghost which they called the brown lady. One night after we had all been at the Greyhound, we were joking with one another about her on our way back, and as we came up to the guard, whose name was Jenkins, we said to him 'we think the brown lady will show up tonight so you look out for yourself'. We asked him what he would do if he did see her. He replied 'well you will hear one shot from me and then I shall be gone, you won't see me any more'. As we walked to our quarters we joked to one another about giving him a scare by one of us dressing up as the brown lady but none of us dare do it after he said to us that you will hear one shot. I think we all feared he would shoot us before he ran off so we let the matter drop – probably for the best looking back on it all".

"January 1941, and orders came that we were to leave Raynham Hall and move to a small village called Harpley where we were billeted in the school hall. Not much for us to do here in the way of night life as there was only one small pub, and more times than not it had run out of beer. Our training was very intense now and was very hard work but after only a few days of being here we were ordered to clean up the carriers and make ready to move off again".

Orders came that the whole battalion was to move to Scotland to Dumfries. I was promoted to Sergeant and told that from Dumfries I would be going abroad but was not told where to. It was so very cold on arrival at Scotland and we were put straight into training; very hard work being made to run up and down the hills in full kit. I remember I found a nice little cafe in Dumfries and used to get my egg and chips there. At the time there were a lot of Norwegians there and we found it hard to get on with them, but the Scottish people were great to us and treated us very kindly. I also liked their beer; it was very sweet compared to ours and went down a treat. It was just what we needed after a cold hard day up and down those hills".

"Towards the end of March I was given a week's leave and told to enjoy it as when I got back we were to leave for foreign shores. It made my journey home all the more important to me, and as I sat looking out of the train window I took in all the landscape and could see what a wonderful country I was going to be fighting for. Before I knew it we had arrived at Peterborough station and I changed trains for Ely. I was met by dear Joyce and my family and oh how good it was to see and hold them all again. We all had so much to talk about and I hardly dare tell them that I was going abroad but the week soon went and I said my goodbyes to all my mates who had not gone off to war, and said my goodbyes to Joyce and my family, which really pulled at the old heart strings, I can tell you. As I left Ely station that night I wondered in my heart if I would ever see them all again".

"It was now April 1941, and as I arrived back at Dumfries expecting the big move to those foreign shores, my mates informed me that it was all off. It was a let-down to me as I had built myself up for it, but instead we were moved to Crewe in Cheshire. We were billeted in Crewe town hall and many of the chaps were put into Nissen huts. While here we were given an exercise to attack Crewe! All the local folks from the surrounding villages and the town were told about it and asked to treat it as the real thing, which they did. You should have seen the state of us – we had bags of flour and soot thrown at us, rotten eggs, you name it I think they threw it at us. One chap said 'no wonder the bloody Germans don't invade – their spies must have told them about this lot'. But once we were all cleaned up and off duty we would have a drink and share a laugh about it all with the locals. We often went from here to Wales for more hill training. This time we were given live ammunition to use and alas a few of the Welsh sheep found their way, along with some mint sauce, to the cook house. The Welsh people were also very kind to us and as you know their own lads suffered as much as anyone in the war".

77

"October 1941 arrived and I was given a week's leave and was told once again that this would be my last leave for some time as on return we were going abroad. On the way home I never thought much of it. I had been told this before and nothing had happened, and in my own mind I thought it would be the same again. But this time I was wrong. On my return to camp we were all told that King George VI was coming to inspect us before we left England. We spent the next few days preparing for his visit – so much spit and polish you could nearly see your face in the carriers. On the day he was to arrive we all had to line up on both sides of the main road and, yes, he did arrive and inspected us. Once he left we were all ordered to prepare to break camp and make ready to leave for Scotland again, this time to Gourock, where we boarded a Polish ship called the Sobuski and on the 31st of October we set off for Halifax, Nova Scotia".

"After we were about one day out the seas turned so rough that you could not even see our escort ships. We were zig-zagging about to try and dodge the Nazi U boats but I think we were being thrown about so much that they need not have bothered with the zig zagging. There were pails and tin baths put out for us all to be sick in. I think it fair to say about 90% of us were very sick and bad and never left our beds for days. There was plenty of food but none of us could eat it as we all felt so ill. It was so good to reach Halifax and get on firm ground again for a while. Here we were put on to an American liner, the Mount Vernon – such a large ship that we all travelled much better and we were soon eating again – some of the best food I have ever eaten. Those Americans really do know how to eat well".

"As I had passed all the P.T. courses the army had sent me on, it was now time to earn my extra pay. I was given a party of men and told to put them through their paces to keep them fit but sometimes it was all we could do to stand up let alone run about. I tried to make it as much fun as I could for the lads and if nothing else I think we all had a good laugh. We were given lectures on war fare etc. and told we were heading for Trinidad. We arrived on the 17th November and stayed for two days. None of us were allowed to go ashore and on the 19th we set off again, this time we were told we were heading for South Africa. This was a long journey and we thought we would never get there. We did not see land for many weeks and as this was the first time most of us had ever left dear old England; it was very worrying to us land lovers. I kept myself busy taking the lads for P.T. and arranging boxing matches during which I found myself in the ring more often than not, getting my self knocked about from some chap from one of the other companies, but it was all good fun and helped take your mind off things and helped the time pass quickly".

"At last we arrived at Cape Town, South Africa on the 13th December 1941. We were now allowed ashore – something we were so glad of – and the local people were all so kind to us. They took us home to tea with them, took us for a beer and showed us around the sights. I had many photos taken with them and enjoyed my four days here very much".

"On the 18th December we set sail again, this time for Bombay, but after a few days out we received orders to turn around and sail for Mombasa, East Africa. We arrived here on Christmas Day 1941. It was so very hot here and we were sweating buckets; we were told to keep our fluid intake up of course. There's always some joker and he said 'get us to the nearest pub then, mate, and let's get some pints down us'. We were allowed ashore after being warned about certain things not to do. Buses were laid on for us and they took us to some wonderfully beautiful beaches where we swam in an attempt to keep cool but some of the chaps got very badly sunburnt – they really were covered in bad blisters and this spoilt the stay here for them. Those of us that were OK took in the sights – and we could buy a great bowl of fruit for 6d! After we had seen enough we would hire a rickshaw each and place bets on which of us would get back to the ship first. Once back on board we would lay up on deck eating our fruit. One of my mates at the time, a Sergeant Bailey, would always say 'this is the life mate; this is how the other half live you know. If our King George could see us now he would be proud of us lads'. If we ran out of fruit we would pay one of the local lads a penny and off he would go and bring us back another tanners worth. The only bad thing that happened here was that we got no Christmas dinner as the fridges packed up and the chefs found all the turkeys etc. had gone off so these were all fed to the sharks, but at least they looked as if they enjoyed them. We didn't mind too much, though, as we had so much fruit to eat and it was so hot that not many of us fancied hot food anyway".

"On the 29th December we left Mombasa. We were told we were heading for Singapore – yes, the impregnable fortress that we had heard so much about. No need to worry now, we were told, so many big guns pointing out to sea that nothing will get into Singapore if it is not wanted. Oh how wrong they were. We stopped one day at the Maldive Islands but never went ashore as we were being given so many lectures now on jungle warfare".

"We were told that the Japanese could not even see more than 10' in front of them because of the way their eyes were slanted, and that

they knew nothing about jungle warfare and that they would not dare
come through the jungle to Singapore so we had nothing to worry about.
We would merely be a deterrent force. We believed all this at the time,
for we believed our intelligence chaps were the best there was in the
world, but we soon found out that the Japanese could teach them a
thing or two".

"I was given more P.T. to take in a last attempt to get the men fit
and most of us were in good shape now and felt ready for some action.
We had trained so much over the last couple of years, we wanted to see
if it would be to good effect".

"We arrived at Singapore on the 13th January 1942. It was raining
so hard that you could hardly see in front of you. We disembarked on
the 14th and were given tents to put up which was utter chaos in such
conditions. I was given orders to make for Malaya as the Japs were moving down fast now. When I got to the causeway I was told there weren't
enough carriers and I was to go back to guard the ammo dumps until
the other carriers arrived, which of course they never did".

"I was put in charge of transport for delivering the ammo to our
units and one day Sergeant Bailey came to me and said 'goodbye Percy
old mate, I don't think I shall ever see you again as I am moving up now
to Malaya'. I said 'well I shall see you when it's all over, mate, so don't
worry'. He looked at me and he gripped my hand and said 'something
tells me I won't make it' to which I replied 'don't talk daft', but alas he
was right and he was killed. In the next few days I was to find out just
what it was like in the heat of battle as our Colonel sent for me and
informed me that he wanted me to take charge of 11th Platoon as the
Officer had been killed, their Sergeant Bert Major had been badly
wounded and their Platoon Officer, Lieutenant Clancey, had been
wounded in the foot. I took off with the platoon and we made our way
up to Malaya. Such fierce fighting took place, it upsets me even now to
think about it. So many good young men just slaughtered to death. I
soon found out that the Japs knew more about jungle warfare than we
had been told about. Some of the traps they set were just horrific – the
way they killed our chaps meant a terrible death. After days of fighting
like this, on the 19th January we were ordered to pull back as the Japs
had now got behind us. I was told to inform my men that it was now
every man for himself and we were all to do our best to get back to base
at Singapore – how we did that was up to us. Those who came with me
were just like me, tired out and afraid. We did our best to travel by night
but there were so many Jap snipers about that we lost many good men.
We passed hundreds of our dead comrades which made us feel sick to

the stomach as many times it would turn out to be one of your own mates. We travelled like this for days until at last we got back to our own lines at Singapore island. Many of the chaps had even made their way down the coast in old boats – for those that made it that way at least they missed the swamps that swallowed up many a good man. We lost so many good men and Officers over those few days".

"Once back at Singapore we had to reorganise and we took up positions on and around the island. We spent our time digging trenches and stocking up with tins of fruit but we were still being told we need not worry as the Japs would not be able to cross the causeway now it had been blown. We took no notice of these things now, as we had seen so many of our mates killed that we knew how good the Japs could fight and I, like most of the others, now followed my own instincts to try and keep alive. We were given no air cover and the Japs had complete control of the air and were bombing us as they liked – we had no chance without air cover and so many more good men were killed. I was given orders to take a party of men to knock out a small building that we were told was occupied by Jap spies who were signalling our positions to the Japs. They would not come out and soon started firing at us so we lobbed in grenades which soon sorted them out. As I entered the building I soon saw the remains of the radio receiver and to those with me I said 'that's for our mates that these scum have killed'. I fear we had been too late though for as we left the building one of the chaps with me was picked off by a Jap sniper right through his head. He never knew what hit him but at least it was quick. We were losing so many men because of these snipers and I felt responsible for my men. I was only 21 years old and I think when you are seeing death all around you at that age after how I had been brought up in England with love and care of your fellow men, I think it fair to say I was in a state of shock at seeing so much death. We soon found out that the Japs had got behind us yet again and we were all feeling so tired that at night as you looked out at the rubber trees you thought they were the Japs advancing towards you, and men would start to fire at the trees in panic. The Japs would call out 'help, help' in good English voices trying to trick us into thinking they were our own boys laying wounded in the hope that we would venture out to try and collect our wounded. At first some of the chaps fell for it but after so many got picked off you soon learnt not to believe what you were hearing".

"There was so much death around now that lorries were collecting the dead all the time – not just our own lads but hundreds of locals killed in the air raids. The ack ack guns just never stopped and the

Japanese planes were just picking us off at will. We were told we would be receiving no more help and that it was now expected that every man would fight to the death, which may sound daft but we were all so worked up that we were all prepared to do this. We were changing positions all the time now and I remember one of the last places that I was dug in was on the top of a hill overlooking the main road. The Japs had us pinned in and they were swimming across the causeway now that the bridge had been blown. They were also behind us – coming at us from every direction. As we ran out of ammo we took them on hand to hand. The only trouble with this was that they were not afraid to die and it's very hard to fight someone who has no fear of death when all you want to do is stay alive. So many men were dying all around me now and as I finished standing up to one Jap charge, I was looking around me at our dead when a voice said 'mind out the way Sarge, let us through, this chap's still alive'. As I looked down at the chap on the stretcher I saw it was my dear mate Len Gilbey – his arm had been blown off. I smiled at him and said 'you will be OK Len. It's over for you now. Our doctors will soon have you mended'. But as they carried him off it hit me hard to see my best mate in such a state. I think when the next charge of Japs came at us I took many of them out through my anger at what they had done to Len".

"We only had one bren carrier now, driven by a chap called Nichols. He had picked me up and brought me up to my position. I had been carrying everything I owned on my back including all the gifts that I had brought on our way out and the photos of those good people I had met. Nichols said to me 'Sarge, you can't keep carrying that lot about on you, it will slow you down too much. Leave it with me in the carrier. I'll look after it for you'. This is what I did and after days of this fighting when I at last pulled back, I passed the remains of the carrier and found that the Japs had stopped it. They gave Nichols no chance – just lobbed in grenades and burnt him alive and of course all my belongings went up with him, God rest him".

"All hell was let loose now – everything that could fire did so and if we could not get ammo then we fought with our bare hands. So many of my best mates from the Cambridgeshire's died – they gave it their best and had done what had been asked of them. The smell of death hung over the whole of Singapore but by some miracle I was still alive. I tried to make my way back to HQ with the chaps that were still with me. On our way we met up with a Corporal Green who asked where we were heading for. I told him 'back to HQ to help them'. He said 'you don't need to go any further. They've all been wiped out, Sarge. We've had it.

There's too many of them for us to beat now Sarge. They've got control of the island. There's no water, they've turned it all off. So it really is every man for himself now Sarge'. I looked at the men with me and said 'you've heard what Corporal Green has to say. They've wiped out HQ so let's get out of here and head for the jungle', which we did. On our way we were passing heaps of dead people, mainly Chinese. You could see how they had been slaughtered to death by the Japs and I think this made us even more determined not to let them take us".

"After a couple of days we were informed that we had surrendered. It was Sunday 15th February 1942. We were told to damage our rifles and lay them in a pile on the side of the road. We all made sure they would not fire again. I think it fair to say that all of us just fell down and went to sleep for we had not slept for days and all of us were so tired. We were awoken by Japanese and after they had taken from us anything they thought would be of help to them, we were rounded up and lined up ready to march off to Changi jail. The thing I remember most was how we all felt so let down. If only we had been given air and navy support we felt sure there would have been a different outcome. Yes, we really were the forgotten army – thrown into a lost cause, with so many good young lives just wasted".

"We were soon to learn how much the Japs hated us as we set off to march the 17 miles to Changi jail. Those that had been wounded were finding it hard to keep up and the Japs took great delight in hitting out at them. I saw many a chap get his head split open by the end of a rifle butt and as soon as he fell to the floor the Japs would swarm round him like flies to put the boot in, and many of them were never to make it to Changi. Some people say, looking back, it was lucky for them, for we were now entering into hell on earth for the next three and a half years – I think I knew that just from what I was seeing on this march to Changi. On our arrival at Changi we had to find somewhere to bed down; the place was just packed to the seams. The hospital unit was overflowing and could not cope with all the sick and wounded men that they were now receiving. Men were laying in the corridors because there were no beds or room for them. The next day we received our ration of rice but thank God some of us still had a few tins of corned beef, which we mixed with the rice. The rice smelt just like rotten eggs but it was that or nothing so we ate it. After a week like this the Japanese knew what a work force they had at their command and so we were put into work parties. I was taken to the docks to help clear up etc. There were many piles of dead Chinese all over the place and the smell was sickening. Thankfully we were taken to the docks in lorries at first so as to save our energy for work. We managed to get some tins of fruit which we took back for our sick lads. Some of the Chinese gave us bread but the Japs found out and executed some of them and forced us all to watch. Needless to say, this soon put stop to them giving us anything, so we had to take what we could when we could. One day we found a crate of duck eggs; we each put one under our hats to get them into camp. These were a Godsend to our boys who were sick. So the next day we tried the same but the Jap guards must have realised what we had done for when we arrived back at the camp we were made to line up in the full heat of the sun for about three hours. Many of the lads passed out through the heat after a hard days work, and as they fell of course the eggs broke. As the Japs moved in on them with their big boots the rest of us were pushed and shoved about and hit over the head, then the Japs would laugh as the egg yolk ran down our faces. After this anyone returning to camp wearing a hat was of course hit on the head".

"One day down at the docks, we had finished our work and the Jap guard had left us alone as he was occupying himself with a couple of the local girls. There was an old American car standing near to us and one of the chaps said 'wonder if we could get it going and make a run for it' to which we replied 'what's the use of that, we are on an island, everywhere we went there would be Japs so you can count that one out'. I told him 'we would be better off trying to steal a ship to get away in'. The lads said 'go on though Sarge, see if you can get it going just for a bit of fun. It can't be much different from your old carrier engine'. 'Well,' I said 'you keep a look out for our guard. If he comes back and finds me trying to get it going he is bound to think we are trying to escape and I want to keep my head on my body so if he comes along you shout'. I lifted the bonnet up and started to tinker with the engine. I cleaned up the points and pushed on the leads to the plugs and coil, when I heard the lads shout 'look out Sarge, the Japs are coming'. I jumped up and hit my head on the bonnet and as I looked up I could see that the Japs coming towards me had seen what I was doing. The other lads made out they were lifting boxes on to an old lorry. I knew it would be no good moving away from the car as they had seen me for sure. I kept on working on the engine and soon felt the end of a Japs pickle stick in my back and in pigeon English came a voice saying 'what you do prisoner?' I felt like saying 'you can bloody well see what I'm doing' but I was so scared I really thought this would be my lot for they must have thought I was trying to get it going to escape in. I came out from under the bonnet slowly as he still had his pickle stick in my back. He had two other Japs with him and I feared they would all beat me to death there and then. He said again 'what you do with motor you prisoner?' I replied 'I have been asked to see if I can get the engine to work sir', which was no lie as my lads had asked me to. He replied 'where's your guard then?' I told him 'I think he has gone to see if he can get some parts for the engine'. The sweat was pumping out of me, my heart was thumping so fast and I felt sure he did not believe one word I was telling him and the other two just stood giving me such an evil look I really thought I was for it. When the one doing all the talking said 'will it go then?' I said 'yes, I think it will now'. He replied 'you get going, you be OK'. I looked across at my mates who were all watching to see what would happen to me. One of them smiled across at me and held his hand up – I could see he had his fingers crossed for me and I think I had everything crossed as well as saying a prayer. I got in to the drivers seat and turned the ignition on and pressed the starter button. After what seemed like forever, she started to cough and splutter. I kept pumping the throttle and at last she fired into life, the little Jap was smiling now and he said 'you drive?' I replied 'yes sir'. He then jumped in beside me, the other two got in the back, and he told me to drive. I drove them all round the docks until the one beside me said 'we go back now'. I drove back to where my mates were at the docks and parked up just where the car had been. As we all got out, our guard, who had returned now, came over shouting at the top of his voice. The little Jap who had sat beside me shouted back at him. The guard then bowed to him and said no more. The little Jap, who must have been one of their Officers, then looked at me and said 'I see you here in the morning'. He and the other two then walked off. I feared a beating from our guard but he said nothing at all until he shouted out 'all men back to camp'. As we marched back to camp and met up with other work parties, the lads took great delight in telling the others what I had done. Once back at camp we were given the usual treatment – left to stand for an hour or more while the guards tried to count us, which they never could do. The next day I had no sooner arrived at the docks when this little Jap Officer turned up, on his own this time, carrying a can of petrol which he got one of the chaps to pour in the car's tank. He spoke to our guard then he called to me 'you come now'. As I walked off my mates said 'best of luck Sarge', but it turned out to be my best day spent as a prisoner of the Japs. I drove him all over the island, he spoke very nicely to me and gave me food. I could see what a hold the Japs now had on Singapore – their soldiers were everywhere. But we had no trouble getting by them – they just waved us through and bowed towards us. I laughed to myself and told myself 'that's right you nasty little men. That's how you should bow to me', for back at Changi I was finding out only too well what they were like if you forgot to bow at them. I knew they were not bowing at me but I told myself they were. After a day of sightseeing around Singapore, I drove him back to Changi where he thanked me for driving him and he gave me a big basket of fruit. I thanked him and asked if he would need me tomorrow. I think in my heart I hoped he would say yes but no such luck. He looked at me and said 'no more driving round, I have seen island now' so my chauffeuring days were soon over. I had eaten well that day so I gave some of the fruit to those in the hospital, especially my dear old mate Len. As I walked into the hospital unit, the lads were just having their rice ration and the smell of rotten eggs was very strong. The rice had been treated ready for sowing but the Japs had now decided to feed us with it. We had found some curry powder at the docks and we used to mix some with our rice to spice it up in an attempt to take away the smell. As we mixed in the curry powder it turned blood red and tasted terrible but it was that or nothing and so we ate it. After a few weeks of nothing but this to eat, the men were going to the Medical Officer to say 'Sir I have not opened me bowels for nearly a month, Sir' to which he would say 'try not to worry, give it another few days and if no luck come back and see me'. I went about 14 to 18 days before I went but for most of the chaps in Changi when they did finally go it turned to dysentery and this took many lives. My mate Sergeant Wadlow died like this; he was in my carrier platoon and was one of the best. He died on my birthday, 11th May. He was the first Cambridgeshire to die as a prisoner. As he was my mate I was given charge of his burial detail, which I arranged for the next day, the 12th May. I was sent to the mortuary to collect him and it was then that it hit me – it really did upset me. I had seen so many good blokes blown to bits and killed in the fighting that I thought I would be hardened to death but as I walked in there lay 10 bodies on a table all with a label tied round their necks – other than that they were naked. They looked so thin and their faces twisted in agony. It really got to me and I broke down and cried like a baby. After I got used to the sights that lay before me, I composed myself and prepared my mate for burial". *[Please see detailed plan of Sergeant Wadlow's funeral]*.

"As soon as the burial was over, I was sent back to work at the docks. The Japs were becoming even more cruel now and more and more of us were receiving beatings for the least little thing – just to look at a Jap wrongly was all it took and with me being tall, I soon found they did not like me at all. They made us count in Japanese when we were being counted and if you could not answer back with the right number in

DETAIL FOR FUNERAL - SJT WADLOW

Bearer Party   Sjt Legge and 6 Other Ranks.

Representative Party
                      2 Offrs, 8 Sjts and 22 ORs
Buglar   Griffiths 1 Camb. (if available)

Time Of Burial   1500 hrs 12 May 42.

Arrangements
                Bearer Party Parade at 1400 hrs.
          Bearer Party will proceed to Cemetery Office and
collect flag. Leaving railway line on right they will
proceed to Hospital Mortuary, apply for truck and Union Jack
and return with body along previous route to Singapore Gate
to arrive at 1450 hrs.
          After ceremony Bearer Party will return truck
and Union Jack, finally returning the flag to the
Cemetery Office.

                Reprsentative Party
          Representative Party will parade at 1430 hrs
and proceed to Singapore Gate, where they will meet the
body at 1455 hrs.
          "Slow March" will be given when the Cortege
moves off.

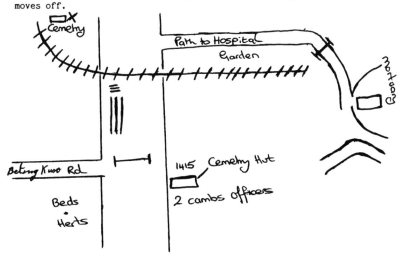

Japanese that was it for you. For example: 1 - Itchi; 2 - Ne; 3 - San; 4 - She; 5 - Go; 6 - Roko; 7 - Isti; 8 - Otchi; 9 - Coo; 10 - Nejou. Most of us would always shout jack, queen, king after 10 but they soon got wise to this and just vented their anger on one of us. I can assure you there is nothing worse than to have to watch a friend beaten and kicked to death by Jap guards knowing that if you stepped forward to help, you would receive the same, or a rifle butt in the face or bayonet to the stomach. It is a sight that stays with you for the rest of your life and the worst thing is they always come back to haunt you in your sleep, even these 50 odd years on, I still can't escape the Japanese nightmares".

"One good thing that did happen at Changi was that my dear friend Len Gilbey recovered and one day when I returned from work I was so pleased to find he had been moved into share the same room as me. I can't tell you how good it was to see his smiling face that day; all those good memories of the fun we had shared while training back in England came flooding back to me. I went straight up to him and embraced him and flung my arms round him. I felt this one arm come round my back and hug me and it was then that I realised he really did have only one arm. I told him 'you will be alright now mate. Now you're with me, I can keep an eye on you'. I knew only too well by now how the Japs picked on those who were disabled and promised him 'as long as I'm about, I won't let them get at you mate' and I like to think I did my best to protect him from them. I used to wash his back for him and as I did so he would say 'wash me arm as well'. He meant the one that he had lost. I would say to him 'come on you old fool, you know you've only got the one arm now' to which he would smile and say 'why does the bloody thing ache so much then if it's not there?' I used to laugh it off and say 'oh stop your moaning or else you can wash your own back', but after all he had suffered he always kept his sense of humour and I am proud to say he was the best mate I ever had".

"Now and again I would be able to bring some coconuts in from the docks and I would grate them up over our rice ration. One day as we sat eating this, Len said to me 'I know where there are some bananas growing and they are hanging over enough for us to reach them if we want to'. So that night we crept out, not telling anyone, but when we got to where the bananas were growing, I could see we couldn't reach them so I got Len to stand on my shoulders. But as he only had the one arm he couldn't balance and get the bananas as well so he said 'you stand on my shoulders'. Good job no one could see us for we were both laughing but after some effort I managed to stay on his shoulders and get the bananas. Just as we had gathered them up we heard voices and we crawled under some nearby bushes to hide. There were a couple of Jap guards who had stopped for a cigarette and a chat, but we knew if they saw us it would be curtains for us. I said to Len 'don't you sneeze now mate or we are dead ducks'. He started laughing and I thought we'd had it for sure. I said to him 'shut up – they're going to hear you' but as I did the Japs moved off and we then both sat and laughed. 'What a couple of fools – we are risking our lives for a few bananas' I said to him, but that was how desperate we were to get something better to have with our rice. Once we got ourselves together we made our way back and hid the bananas in a box under our beds. They weren't ripe but after a few days they soon ripened and we enjoyed them together. I think it helped keep us going and with the things I managed to bring back from the docks it kept us alive at that time, for all around us now men were dying from starvation and dysentery etc".

"I was sent with some of the others to clear another part of jungle to make the cemetery bigger as the death rate was very high now. June 1942 came and the Japs had us all parade in the main square where once again we were left to stand in the full heat of the sun for hours before the camp commandant finally came out, by which time many of the men had collapsed through heat exhaustion. Those of us left standing were informed 'no more men die now; we take you to Thailand to good hospital camps where you plenty food, lots good music and you all relax and get fit and be happy' ".

"Len was not picked to go – he was to stay at Changi for the rest of his days as a prisoner. I was very upset at having to leave him. 'Who's going to look out for you now and keep you out of trouble?' I said. It was a very emotional farewell and in my heart I really thought he would not make it through without me. The next day we were marched off to the station carrying everything we had to our names, which was not much. We were loaded into steel sided cattle trucks, thirty or more to each one – nowhere to lay, hot, and flies everywhere. We travelled like this for over five days and nights stopping only once a day at one of the stations to be given some cold rice and a drink of muddy water. They would shout at us 'Speedo hurry Banjo toilet' but most of the lads were too ill to make it to the toilet – so you can imagine the stench in the trucks. Most of us were suffering from dysentery and we used to have to hold one another out of the doors of the trucks by holding them at arms length. There was the odd case of men not being strong enough to hold on to the chap and they fell to their deaths. There was no chance of stopping for them and they were left where they fell. Their death would be recorded as 'died from dysentery' but over the months of the Japs moving us men like this I wonder just how many men met their death like this; most of the men who were prisoners on the death railway have seen someone die in this way. We arrived at the first camp called Ban Pong. We could see it was a hell hole – 'so much for holiday camps' we said to one another. One chap said 'yeah, I think that's what Changi was compared to this'. We waded up to our waists at times in the camp – it was just a quagmire – sewage was floating around and the stench in the camp was enough to make you reach. There were a few old atap huts with decaying roofs and inside them there were wooden platforms, thank God, about 2' off the ground and if you were lucky the part you slept on was just above the water but there were so many bugs at night that you felt you were being eaten alive. We also had to watch out for snakes that would swim in the swamp-like conditions for we had no vaccine or anti-dotes for anyone who did get bitten. There were maggots everywhere so no wonder there were so many flies – it really was hell on earth. Our Officers asked the Japs for better conditions but were soon told 'you no complain, you prisoners, you here to build railway'. We soon found out that our lives meant nothing to them, but the conditions were so bad that they did move some of the men to higher ground to keep them dry – the only trouble was these poor men were already dead. 'That's the only way to get out of here' chaps would say when they carry you out, 'that's the only time we shall get on dry ground'. We built new huts with timber we cut from the jungle and covered the roofs with jungle foliage. When it came to eat our rice, we would collect it then wade back to our beds and sit on them to eat it, but you only got enough for about five mouthfuls so it did not take long. I think we all knew that the stench and conditions we were having to eat and live in was going to kill us all in time unless we could get away".

"I soon went down with malaria and felt so ill but I was lucky and came through it OK. Once I was a bit better I was sent to work near Kanchanaburi, cutting back the jungle. We also cleared a large area to use as a cemetery as we were told 'many men coming from Singapore'. We thought they meant these men were already dead and they were just bringing them here to bury them, but they were all alive and we soon realised the Japs knew that so many of them would arrive dead or die soon after they arrived at the conditions they were to face at Ban Pong".

"Once we had finished building the huts and clearing jungle back for the cemetery, we were informed by the Japs that we were now to be moved up to Tamarkan, and once again we were put to work building huts and clearing back jungle. We had lost some very good men on the march to Tamarkan and we all felt so ill and so low in spirits. We were not allowed any time to rest but put to work straight away on our arrival with cries of 'Speed O' from the Japs all the time. If they thought anyone was not working hard enough then they soon laid into him. Once again I was to lose mates who were beaten to death by these guards all because they were too ill and weak to work, so the Japs just murdered them. The work was getting so hard now – or we were getting weaker – it was one or the other, the latter I think".

"Once we had built enough huts we were moved on again, this time we were told by the Japs that we were going to a place called Chunki. Once again we followed the old elephant tracks through the jungle. It was a very hard march and we lost many more good men. We were all so sick now with dysentery and malaria attacks and we also feared scratching ourselves on bamboo because this would cause a tropical ulcer which just ate your flesh away. Those of us that did make it were soon put to work building huts again – we knew as soon as we got one built, we would have somewhere to rest.... and, oh, how we loved to hear the Japs call Yasume (means rest) – it was music to our ears. Until we had huts built we just had to sleep outside in the open, and I think every bug alive used to try and eat us alive. One day while here a large company of Japanese fighting soldiers arrived. Just by chance one of the guards brought their Officer to me. I couldn't make out what they were talking about as they stood in front of me but I could make out that every now and then the guard would say 'Sergeant' and point to me. After all their nattering the guard hit me with his rifle butt in the stomach; I fell to the floor and rolled into a ball to try and protect myself from the beating that I expected to follow but as he went to kick out at me, the Jap Officer shouted at him. He stopped kicking out at me and stepped back from me. I stayed rolled up tight in a ball, wondering what was to happen now, when the Officer walked up to where I lay and in perfect English said 'don't worry, you get up now and come with me'. I looked up at him and he reached out his arm to help me up. As I stood up I felt terrible and he could see I was shaking, more with fear I think for I still expected the worst. He turned to the guard and shouted something to him and the guard sloped off and vented his anger on one of the other poor chaps".

"The Officer said to me 'you take your time Sergeant, you be OK now, I have job for you to do'. He walked me over to where we had just finished building a hut, looked at me and said 'here you make kitchen, you be my cook and for my men'. I wondered whether to tell him that I was no cook but did not dare. He said 'I show you how to cook my rice. You pick 10 men to help you and all do as I say, you be OK'. The soldiers brought in big coppers for us to cook the rice in, and one copper to keep for making tea in. I picked 10 mates to help me and we set up our kitchen. It saved my life at that time for I had lost so much weight and was feeling so ill that I don't' think I could have protected myself from the guards much more. Seems funny but I think that Jap Officer saved my life that day".

"One morning as we were cooking the rice for them, the Jap Officer came to me and said 'I have lots of boxes coming. You take charge of them and store them for me. If any dami dami (meaning damaged) you must tell me'. The next day these large crates arrived and he and his soldiers brought them all to the kitchen. The Officer told me 'you store, you open, tell me if dami dami'. I bowed to him and said 'yes Sir' to which he looked at the Jap soldiers with him and said 'Sergeant good man' and turned and left. Once they had gone the other lads said 'you're a good man all right Sarge. There must be lots of them damaged you know'. I laughed at them and said 'well if they ain't they soon will be'. We set to and opened the crates, they were full of tins of food, meat and fruit etc. Our eyes lit up and our mouths watered. We already knew how lucky we were not having to work on the railway and were already eating much better quality rice than the other lads as we were eating the same rice we were cooking for the Japs. I said to the lads 'we must be careful here boys. If we go too mad we will blow it and be back on the railway work' and as I say we knew at this time we were so lucky. The next morning the Jap Officer came to me and said 'I have food from tins now mixed with rice for myself and my men'. I bowed again to him and said 'yes Sir'. He asked me if 'any tins dami dami?' I replied 'yes'. His face turned sour looking and he said 'you must show me'. I took him to where we had damaged a few of the tins by denting them – we had also already opened one and filled it with slop that smelt terrible. I showed him the dented tins then the slop tin. As I did so, I held my nose and said 'gone bad'. He soon stepped back from the smell of it. He looked at me and said 'you only use good food for me, you check all tins before you cook'. I replied 'oh yes Sir, of course I will. I won't let you have any bad food'. I bowed to him and he said 'you good man'. He then turned and left. I told the others to get some of the tins hidden out of the way and from out of the kitchen and hide them up in our hut, which they did, then at night once our work was done, we would have a feast. We made sure also that the boys in the sick hut received a share of it as by now the Japs were saying 'no work, no food'. Yes, that one Jap Officer and his soldiers coming to our camp at that time had saved our lives. He allowed myself and the lads helping me to swim in the river and after a days cooking it was such good fun to freshen up with a swim and splash about with your mates. I think it fair to say it was to be the best time of my captivity. I and the others with me even put some weight back on again. Then one day the Jap Officer came to our kitchen and told me he and his men were leaving. He thanked us for looking after him and his men so well to which we all thought 'no, thank *you*, mate, for looking after *us*' for we all knew how much better we were feeling. Once they had left, the camp guards soon started at us and my days of being a cook were over. They took all the food that was left but not before my lads had made sure we had tins stocked up for our own use. We were put straight back on to building the railway. It came so hard to us as we were given the job of carrying the crushed rocks in baskets to use as ballast for the railway embankment. It was a long hard day now of up to 16 hours – the Japs even set up acetylene gas lights so that we could work through the night".

"We soon lost the weight we had put on while being cooks, but we did have our tins of meat well hidden and it was this that was keeping us alive. We treated it like gold dust and mixed a little with our rice slop each night, but the work was so hard that we burned up energy so fast and I soon started to get run down again. And without those extra vitamins I soon got leg ulcers – most of the lads did. We knew how quick you could lose a leg because of them – or even die. We had no medication for them and all our Medical Officer had was something called blue stone powder which would help dry it up and form a scab, if you were lucky. Sometimes we would put on maggots to eat the poison out then after a time we would stand in the river and let the little fish eat out the maggots, then the Medical Officer would put some more blue stone on it in the hope that it would scab. It was all you could do to walk with the pain of them, but the Japs still made sure you did your days work. If they thought you were slacking they would kick you on your ulcer. You can imagine the pain from this, let alone the damage it could do in making the ulcer spread, and I know many men who lost a leg from the result of such treatment, most of them from the operation, or if not, a few days later, for we just did not have the proper aftercare for them. For those that did survive they were just so very lucky".

"The rice we were being fed on now was just so bad it was like water. We all had such bad dysentery as by now all our tins of food had gone and we were trying to eat anything to try and stay alive – snakes, rats, insects, even small monkeys – that is if we could catch them. Then one day the Japs told us 'new rice supply come, you unload it, put in store'. It was all we could do between us to lift a sack of it. Once it was used up the Japs made us make stretchers out of them by inserting bamboo poles along each side of them, we thought they were to carry our sick men on, but soon found out that it was to lift rocks. With one of us on each end, the Japs would make sure that far too much was loaded onto them and then laugh at us as we tried to carry them. We knew what would happen if we fell down and dropped them and this is just what the Japs wanted to happen, and it was often the end for those who did fall – the guards were on them in a flash, putting their boots and rifle butts in until the bloke moved no more. Then, and only then, were we allowed to use the stretcher to carry a body. We were in such a bad state now with attacks of malaria and dysentery that I knew the work was going to kill me, the food was getting less and I thought it would only be a matter of time until I took that final beating".

"Then on the 25th November 1942 I was told I was being moved to camp Wun-towkien, further up the line. I was not sad at leaving Chunki as I knew if I did not get away I would die there. As we left camp that day we looked just like walking skeletons but just the rest from lifting rocks for 16 hours a day helped our bodies a little. We soon arrived at Wun-towkien and were allowed a day to rest. I think they could see we were dead on our feet but early next morning we were taken out to work on the railway. Over the next few days four of the chaps that had helped me cook for the Japs fell dead. As I lay on my bed that night, I was so bad with malaria that I really thought I was dying myself. Then I saw my dear Joyce's face saying to me 'come on Percy. Don't you let these so and so's kill you. I need you to come home to me, for I love you so much'. I know it sounds daft but it saved my life. I knew she came to me that night and gave me the strength to come through. The next day I was too ill to parade for work in the fit-for-work line and so had to be pushed and shoved about by the guards to make sure I was not malingering. They pushed me to the floor and said 'man no good'. My mates laid me back on my bed and went off to work. Later that day I was sent back to Chunki – 'to the hospital' (the Japs said), but all it was was just another old atap hut. I remember thinking to myself how much I wanted to get away from Chunki and now here I was being brought back to die. I had 21 other chaps with me who had been sent back with me, and more than half of them were to lose their lives in this hut. I was lucky I did have a little money that I had kept hidden, and was able to get one of my mates to buy me some duck eggs which I am sure helped me to recover. They tasted just like fish though, and once i was up and about again I was to find out why. All the local natives fed the ducks on their fish scraps and with the ducks eating nothing but fish I can only imag-

ine that this caused them to smell so much like fish but they helped me
to get a little fitter and got me out of the death hut. It was the 1st of
January 1943 when I came out of this hut – a new year, and oh how I
prayed it would be a good year when we would be set free. It was with
this hope in my heart that I started back to work on the railway that day.
They treated me like a dog, though, and I knew if I was to survive I had
to get a move. It came in the middle of January, when I was moved to
Takiren but here we were made to work in the full heat of the sun, and
at midday it was just unbearable, and the food was so very bad that I
soon got sick again. It was on the 10th February that I went down with
malaria again and beri-beri".

"I spent a long while in the hospital hut this time and once again
thought my time had come. The two chaps laying either side of me died
within minutes of one another and I thought I would join them at any
time. It became hard to fight against it, for it felt so easy to just give up
and slip away but my mates would visit me and say 'come on Percy, hang
on in there mate'. They would bring a duck egg for me or a banana, and
they would make sure I ate them. I know I owe them for keeping me
alive at that time and thank God I started to pick up again. I was so
weak, though, and had to be taken to the toilet by two of the stronger
men. The toilet was a trench of about 8' long x 4' wide with a bamboo
pole each side of the trench to sit on, you then had to hold on to the two
stronger men's arms because if you fell into the trench that was your lot.
There was always about 2' at the bottom of human effluent, then another 2' of maggots; the stench was terrible and flies were everywhere. I
can remember gripping the arms of those blokes so tight, I could feel
their arm bones, but thank God they did not let me fall in. I know that
when the war was over these latrines became the graves of a few of the
camp guards. Once I was a bit stronger I had my fair share of holding
onto someone while they went to the toilet. It reminded me of our first
train journey to Ban Pong when we had to hold one another out of the
door. We only had jungle leaves to use as toilet paper – what a state we
were in. A few days before I was fit enough to leave the sick hut, the Jap
guards came in one morning to demand men for work. I just lay still in
the hope they would not pick on me. One poor chap near me, whom I
had befriended, was just like skin and bone; they told him to get up, but
try as he may the poor chap just could not. We moved to try and help
him but were pushed back down. At last he managed to get to his feet
and at once the Jap pushed him back down then they shouted at him to
get up again. They were laughing at him and as he got about half way
up again he just gave out a big sigh and fell back on his bed. Yes, he was

dead but the Japs found this very funny and just laughed to one another. I knew by now what animals they were, but once again I just witnessed them murder someone. Thank God they left the hut then but many more died that day because of the extra stress they had caused. I thanked God that I came out of there alive, I can tell you. I started back to work and thanks to the other lads looking out for me, started to get on a bit better. We were now given one day off and we would boil our clothes – in my case my shorts and rice sack. It was the only way we could kill the lice and bugs, but as soon as we slept that night they were infected again and you could feel the bugs eating at you as you tried to sleep – they were about the size of a ladybird. Although we were in such a bad state, the chaps always kept their sense of humour. When it would be time to go and collect your rice, you would call your mates and hear them reply 'oh I won't be long old boy, I'm just relaxing in the bath' or 'I'm just feeding my horse' or 'make mine roast chicken or fillet steak – I'll get the wine' to which they would reply 'come on you daft bugger', but thank God they did say these things for it brought that touch of humanity to our lives and kept us all in touch with how life used to be".

"March 1943 had now arrived and somehow I was still alive. On the 13th of March I went down with malaria again. I think my body had started to get used to these attacks now and thankfully it only lasted a few days so I was not in the death hut for long, but still each morning the Jap guards came round to try and make you go out to work. I remember as soon as I felt that bit stronger, I said to the chap laying next to me 'I can't stand much more of this every day. I think tomorrow when the guards come for men to work, I shall get up and go into the fit-for-work party as I think it might save them from knocking us about', to which he replied 'yes but you know you won't win if you stop them from beating you here. Once they get you out to work you can be sure one of them will notice that you are not too well and pick on you'. I replied 'yes, but at least you have more chance of keeping out of the way if you keep your head down and keep working – but here they pick on us every day. We are just sitting ducks for them'. He said 'oh, alright – tomorrow we will join the fit parade'. That morning I awoke and rolled off my bamboo platform. I had no clothes by now, just my Jap happy – no boots, not even a hat to keep the sun off my head. As I stood up and had a stretch, I said to the chap 'come on then mate up you get, let's go and get some rice and then we shall be ready to take on the days work'. He never answered me so I walked round to his side and put my hand on his shoulder to shake him but as soon as I did this I could feel how cold he was and knew at once that he was dead. For him the fear of the Japs was over; no more work or worry for him. I rolled him over and laid him flat. His eyes were staring straight at me. I closed them and said 'goodbye old mate'. I then walked out of that death hut saying to myself 'I must not end up in here again'. What hit me most was that the night before, he had said he felt OK and was pleased to be going out of the death hut tomorrow. Well he did come out of it but not the way he would have liked to I'm sure. I joined the rice queue and met up with my mates again. They told me 'you wait till you see this new rice that the Japs are giving us – it's 30% rice and 70% maggots" and when I got my tin full of it they were right – it was alive with maggots. They said 'just pick the black bits out because they are rat turds'. They gave us what they called stew to have with it but it was more like muddy water. Our Medical Officer told us to eat the lot – he said 'the maggots will have lots of protein in and do you good'. I thought to myself 'my God, what have we come to, eating bloody maggots', but when it's all there is, you take it. I went off to work that day and thanks to my mates, managed to avoid a beating. Some local Thai's came by wanting to trade but all I had left to my name was my knife, fork and spoon. I knew that now all I would need was my spoon to get the slop down me and so decided to sell the knife and fork. The only other thing I had was my razor and I promised myself I would never part with it. With the little bit of money I got for them, I bought some ducks eggs and bananas – they always were our life savers and oh how good they tasted".

"Towards the end of March things were getting so bad that we decided that a few of us would try and escape in the hope of letting the outside world know of how the Japs were treating prisoners of war. We thought it better that only four of us went – we knew the repercussions it would bring for the chaps left behind but we felt that if we didn't try then no one would know of how we were treated as none of us would be left alive to tell".

"Our escape party was to be C/Sergeant Hicks, Sergeant Newman, Sergeant Kerr and myself. Hicks and Norman were regular soldiers who had been fighting in Malaya long before we had arrived in Singapore. We planned when and where we would make our escape and managed to obtain some maps and a compass. We got together whatever food we could and had prepared our minds for going. Then on the evening before we were to go, one of our Officers came to us and said 'chaps, I don't want to be the one to spoil things for you, but I would like to see you all stay alive. I have been in a couple of camps where men have tried to escape, only to be turned in by the locals for reward and you chaps look all in to me. You're not fit enough to survive in that jungle. I

97

don't think you will be able to help any of us, yourselves included. I don't want to see you being brought back here in a few days beaten near to death, only to have to stand and watch you all beheaded; then I'll have to look at your heads every day when they are shoved on poles in the parade square and you know you're not all that good looking chaps so please don't put me through that torture'. We took in what he had said and thought how right he was. We told ourselves it would be very hard even for fully fit men to survive living off the jungle, and most of us had already lost half our body weight, so we called off our escape attempt".

"It was May 1943 on the seventh day that I received my first letter from home – four days before my birthday. What a birthday present! Some of the chaps were lucky and received two – but these had all been written more than two years before, and the Japs had just not bothered to give them to us. It was a thing I shall never forget – we all just froze to the spot as we read our letters. We all had tears running down our faces – many of the chaps really broke down. I can't tell you how many times I read my letter that day and over the next few weeks – oh, what a tonic it was. I smelt it, tasted it, for it was from my darling Joyce and my family, and to know they were alright was all I needed to help me keep going. We knew that over two years had passed since they had written them and that a lot can happen in two years. 'Just look at the state of us' one chap said, but I knew that my Joyce and family would be safe. I knew it would take more than a few Germans to take over the people of the fens and as I slept that night with my letter held tight in my hand, I thanked God for bringing her words to me. I soon fell asleep in my dreams of home".

"It was not long after this that we were all called out on parade to have the Jap Commandant inform us that 'all fit men have to go on long march, only sick can stay'. He informed us we were going to Takanun. 'It will take you six days' he said. Once again he told us all the lies of how much better the camp would be with plenty of good food and drink and lots of music. We knew by now that none of this would be true and we just hoped we would make it there alive. We also worried for the sick lads that we were to leave behind, for in our minds we thought that once we were gone the Japs would kill them for if you were sick and did not work you received no food, and we knew that without us to share our food with them, they would die. In the course of time, we found out that this is just what happened to them".

"As we marched out of that camp I just kept telling myself 'I will make it'. I read my letter one more time and got my mind prepared to face all that was to come. After the first few days, what had started out as a tightly bunched column of men, was now a well stretched-out line, the weaker men falling way behind. Many of them we were never to see again and to this day I would imagine many of them still lay where they fell. The Japs had a very cruel manner. One chap in front of me was so done in that he fell down which was unlucky for him because a Jap guard was right near to us. Before any of us could help him up, this Jap moved in and said 'I help man up', which he did. The poor chap looked so pleased and as he stood up he smiled at the Jap and bowed down a bit to him. This Jap then smashed his rifle butt down on the back of the poor chap's head, splitting the back of his skull wide open and the chap fell down. Many of us moved towards the guard in our anger, but he quickly turned his rifle at us with his bayonet at the ready. In a flash, other guards were on us shouting 'Speed O, keep moving' – for the poor chap, his hell on earth was over. We carried on, knowing that if we didn't, we would receive the same. Whatever had we done to deserve this treatment? We were mostly young men of just 22 or 24 years old – what *had* we done to deserve this?"

"One evening we arrived at a large rock face with water cascading down it in to the river below. The Japs allowed us to wash under the stream of water so we all stripped off and stood under it. It was so relaxing, as it fell over your tired body. Some local native girls were watching and laughing at us but not one of us cared. One bloke said 'if I could catch one of them I don't think I would be any good to her anyway'. We told him he must be feeling better than most of us to be able to think of such things. It was so good to feel that fresh cool water on you though, and I think most of us had a good drink of it as well. We finally arrived at Takanun after eight days and were soon put to work. The Jap Engineers told us 'you must work hard now, railway must be finished'. We did our best to slow it up as much as we could by using soft wood where we could instead of ballast in the hope that when a train passed by, it would sink in and be derailed but the Japs were watching us so closely that it was hard to get the chance to do much sabotage".

"On the 6th June malaria hit me again and I was put in the hospital hut. I realised that I still had the binoculars and compass that we were going to use on our escape and once I got out of the hospital hut I found a Thai trader and tried to sell them. He took the binoculars but told me 'the compass not working'. He thought it was a watch, and try as I may I could not get through to him. Once again with the money I made I bought some duck eggs, and the next day I found another trader who bought my compass for a few dollars. My mate Sergeant Ager and

I used to pool our money and once we had enough we would buy a tin of thick sweet milk. It tasted so good. We would take two good spoonful's of it after our rice slop each day. One day, when I went to try and get some more of this milk, the Thai trader said 'no more left but I have sweet grease' – it was black and in five gallon cans. I tried some and it was very sweet so I bought a tin although it was all I could do to lift it back to camp, but I managed to make it and get it by the Japs. I told my mate 'I've got an idea how we can make some money for food' so we went to the cook house hut and scrounged all the burnt rice they had and boiled it up in an old can – it looked just like coffee. I shouted out 'come and get it, good cheap coffee'. The lads soon came running with their mess tins. '5 cents a time,' I said. I added a spoonful of the black sweet grease and the chaps loved it. They all said 'where did you get this coffee from, Percy, it's really good?' I told them 'don't you worry where it came from, you just give me your 5 cents and enjoy it'. Once I made some money I bought some eggs and some coconut oil to cook them in and found a quiet little corner at the rear of the hut, and set myself up cooking eggs and making coffee. I was soon making a few dollars and providing a good service. For once the Japs turned a blind eye, thank God. One day after work I set up my little cafe when a new party of men arrived at camp. I was frying up eggs and one of these chaps came over and said 'I didn't think I would see a stallholder here, it's like being back at Ely market'. Once I heard the word 'Ely' I knew he must be a Cambridgeshire chap so I turned round and found it was a chap I had known back home – George Street. I don't think he recognised me as I had a full beard now as I had no razor blades left, but we soon got chatting of home and of all our dear mates that we had lost. He said 'I shall know where to come for me tea then mate' and off he went to get to know the ins and outs of the camp".

"When the Japs allowed us to swim and wash in the river, I and many of the others would tie a piece of wire on the end of a bit of string. We would have the piece of wire bent and sharpened to a point, throw it in and pull it out quickly and 9 times out of 10 you would have a small fish on the end of it. We would collect up our catch, then I would fry them up and eat them with our rice. It was this extra food that was keeping most of us alive. One day while we were trying to fish, one of the Jap Engineers came up to us and said 'you want fish?' We feared the worst but replied 'yes please', whereupon he lit a couple of sticks of dynamite and threw them in the river which stunned all the fish and they just floated on the top. We quickly swam in and collected them up. We had so many of them. The Jap took his fair share and went. We got our catch back to camp and I fried them all up and took most of them to the boys in the sick hut. 'Come on lads,' I said 'have some nice whitebait'. Many of them were now sick and had been my customers and they said 'bring us a cup of your coffee to wash it down with Sarge', which I was only too pleased to do, for it was so important for them to try and eat and drink. I had been glad of the chaps that had helped me out when I thought it was all over for me, and I think it fair to say that most of us did all we could to help one another through those nightmare days".

"One day when we went to swim and fish, we could see dead bodies floating in the river. Orders were given 'no man swim now' but within a couple of days cholera had struck our camp. We tried to make charcoal filters from bamboo and rice sacks, and we boiled the water, but men were dying so fast now it was nothing to get up in the morning and at least five or six men lay dead around you. You could be talking to a chap one minute then say 'see you later', and walk away, only to turn round and see that he had collapsed and died – it was that quick. The Japs were now very worried of catching the disease and some of them did, of course. They told us 'good medical supplies come soon'. We had never received any medication from them before so why should we be-lieve them now. We knew it would have to come from far away and knew it would take too long to get here to help us. I think we all thought it was just a matter of time now before we all died from it. I was now given the worst job I have ever had to do – yes, to burn the bodies. We built large bamboo fires then laid the bodies on top. The Japs allowed us a small amount of oil and petrol to get the fire started quickly but as it flared up the bodies would sit up and stare at you – it is still a sight that haunts me to this day. These were men that I had been working with only a couple of days before, and now here they were being cremated by me – it really did get to me. I lost track of just how many I cremated over that time but enough to know that thousands of dear men met their maker from that terrible death. I was only 23 years old at this time and I know I have had to carry those scars with me from that time on".

"My little sideline of running my cafe soon came to an abrupt end now – I lost all my customers for one thing. I soon found myself being moved out of camp and was put into a party of men, making a total of 10 in all, which was taken out into the jungle and given the job of felling trees. We had one crosscut saw and two large axes between the 10 of us, and one hammer and chisel. All the tools were blunt and of course we had nothing to sharpen them on so the work was very hard. Once we had got the tree down we then had to cut it into one metre lengths, split it in two and stack it beside the railway line. Each pile had to be 10 metres long by one metre high – this would be a day's work. We soon found not to do any more or any less for once you started another pile, they made you finish it and it soon became a long way to carry the logs because as we worked our way into the jungle, the further from the railway line we got, which of course made it much further to carry them. It was now late in November 1943 and lots of Jap troops were passing by our camp with lots of horses. As we worked by the railway line we just waved them through, for we knew it would be a one way trip for them and the last train ride they would get".

"On the 2nd December I went down with malaria again. I knew how run down I was but feared going into the hospital hut. I still had a little money left from my days of running the cafe and spent this on duck eggs and fruit as the rice ration was very bad now. I think the duck eggs and sheer willpower got me through this outbreak of malaria. Christmas of 1943 came and went. We tried to make it a special day as we were allowed one day off, but we were so unwell, it was hard to find any Christmas cheer. Many of the chaps said 'why doesn't someone tell the Japs it's meant to be a time of goodwill towards all men?' Everyone shouted at him '*you* tell them'. Then on the 2nd of January 1944 I was given three letters from home – it was like a late Christmas present, and once again gave me such a boost. I had just about worn my first letter out by now as I had read it so much. I don't know how many times I read them over and over, it was so good to know that all my loved ones were safe and that the outside world still existed".

"On the 24th January the medical supplies the Japs had promised so long ago finally arrived and we were given inoculations for plague, cholera etc. but the next day I felt so terrible I thought I was dying. Many of us feared that the Japs had given us a lethal injection to kill us, but after a day or two we started to feel a bit better and realised it had been the effects of the drugs. On the 3rd of February I was given an injection to stop my dysentery and this made me feel much better. We spoke to one another of how if only we had received these medicines earlier then perhaps many of our mates would still be alive. It certainly made me feel that bit better. On the 11th February we were all called out to parade in front of the Jap Commandant; they called it the sick parade. He shouted at us 'all men take clothes of' which did not take me long for all I had was an old bit of rice sack that I tied round my waist. As we stood there like skeletons the Jap doctor came along the line and stood at one end. We then had to take it in turns to pass by him, and after he made you bend over, he pushed a stick of bamboo up your backside. I can still feel the pain from it when I think about it. He said 'you fit, you go over sea'. We had no idea what he meant and just thought his English was bad, but then on 28th February, those of us who had been passed fit were rounded up and marched out of camp. We made our way back down the line, passing through many of the camps we had built on the way up. I think what shocked me most was the size of the cemeteries. I soon got another attack of malaria but thank God it was not as bad as before – perhaps all the inoculations had helped. My mates helped me along for a few days until it cleared up a bit. We arrived back at Chungkai where they wanted me to go into the hospital hut but I remembered only too well how I had promised myself I would not die in that hut. I said 'no, I will be OK now'. Thank God I did, for if not I would have been left at Chungkai as early next morning we broke camp and moved on until we reached Non Pladuk. Here we were allowed to rest and given fish to eat with our rice. We caught snakes and roasted them – they tasted great, and after a few days rest and being able to eat a bit better we felt that much better".

"It was now the middle of April and again malaria and fever hit me, but for the first time I received a full course of quinine tablets and managed to shake it off once more. I was soon back working with my mates and one day our guard allowed us to have a yasume and take a swim in the river. We all worried about cholera after the last swimming we had done, but it looked so inviting so in we went. It felt so good to be refreshed by the water and when one of the chaps said 'oh look, every time we take a bath we get women watching us. Can't a bloke get any privacy. We've got nothing to offer them'. 'You speak for yourself', one of the chaps would say and when we got out, one of these Thai women came up to me and offered me a small cake that looked like a little jelly-type cake. I said 'I have no money' to which she replied, 'you take, I hate Japanese, they kill my family'. She said 'you come tomorrow, I bring you many more.' The lads all pulled my leg about her by saying 'she only wants your body Sarge; you look out', but I did see her the next day and she brought me plenty of cakes which the chaps were only too pleased to help me eat. For the rest of our stay here I got my cakes from her every day – she knew the risk she was taking but she always turned up. Whether she was telling the truth about her hatred of the Japs I don't know, but her cakes helped keep me going at that time and she is another to whom I owe my life".

"On the 16th of May we were paraded again and informed we were to have another injection for cholera – another ½cc – and it did not make me feel so bad this time. The Commandant informed us we were to keep fit now as we were going back to Singapore. We all wondered

STERN ORDERS FOR PRISONERS AT SEA

Below is a facsimile of orders issued to Allied prisoners transported on Japanese prison-ships as promulgated by the Commander of the Prisoner Escort, Navy of the Great Japanese Empire. As may be seen, threat of the death penalty covered such breaches of discipline as 'talking without permission and raising loud voices' and 'using more than two blankets'. The offer of preferential treatment in clause 6 must have provoked smiles from the prisoners – not merely on account of its pigeon-English.

Commander of the Prisoner Escort Navy of the Great Japanese Empire
REGULATIONS FOR PRISONERS

1. The prisoners disobeying the following orders will be punished with immediate death.
a) Those disobeying orders and instructions
b) Those showing a motion of antagonism and raising a sign of opposition
c) Those disordering the regulations by individualism, egoism, thinking only about yourself, rushing for your own goods
d) Those talking without permission and raising loud voices
e) Those walking and moving without order
f) Those carrying unnecessary baggage in embarking
g) Those resisting mutually
h) Those touching the boat's materials, wires, electric lights, tools, switches, etc
i) Those climbing ladder without order
j) Those showing action of running away from the room or boat
k) Those trying to take more meal than given to them
l) Those using more than two blankets
2. Since the boat is not well equipped and inside being narrow, food being scarce and poor you'll feel uncomfortable during the short time on the boat. Those losing patience and disordering the regulation will be heavily punished for the reason of not being able to escort.
3. Be sure to finish your 'Nature's call', evaculate the bowels and urine, before embarking.
4. Meal will be given twice a day. One plate only to one prisoner. The prisoners called by the guard will give out the meal quick as possible and honestly. The remaining prisoners will stay in their places and wait for your plate. Those moving from their places reaching for your plate without order will be heavily punished. Same orders will be applied in handling plates after meal.
5. Toilet will be fixed at the four corners of the room. The buckets and cans will be placed. When filled up a guard will appoint a prisoner. The prisoner called will take the buckets to the centre of the room. The buckets will be pulled up by the derrick and be thrown away. Toilet papers will be given. Everyone must cooperate to make the room sanitary. Those being careless will be punished.
6. Navy of the Great Japanese Empire will not try to punish you all with death. Those obeying all the rules and regulations, and believing the action and purpose of the Japanese Navy, cooperating with Japan in constructing the New order of the Great Asia' which lead to the world's peace will be well treated.

how he thought we were going to keep fit on what they were feeding us on and by how they were treating us, but the thought of going back to Singapore pleased us. I wondered if I would see my best mate Len again at Changi – was he still alive and getting by alright with just his one arm to protect himself with? Oh how I hoped and prayed he was. It was on the 9th of June that we boarded the train to take us back to Singapore, where we arrived on the 12th of June and informed we were to be allowed to rest up for a while. We were given the best bowl of rice that we had seen since we had left Singapore, and we were given a fresh shirt and shorts. They didn't fit, but who cared? It was just so good to have something to wear at last".

"At the beginning of July we were marched down to the docks which was full of boats and ships. Laying on the dockside were large piles of rubber sheets. As we went on board ship we had to carry two of these sheets with us. There were Jap troops coming aboard as well, and they took delight in pushing us about. A few of them spoke a bit of English and they told us 'if Americans sink us, you be first to die'. Once on board we were pushed into the hold which was so very hot. We had heard stories of how prisoners had been taken out to sea and then thrown overboard to the sharks. We feared this would be our fate but a few of the chaps said 'no, they would have just killed us back on the railway if they meant to kill us. They want us for something – that's why they have allowed us to rest up".

"We left Singapore on the 4th July 1944 with 14 other ships in our convoy and four days later on the 8th we arrived at Borneo. We were not allowed ashore but they did allow some of us to come up on deck to get some fresh air. Oh how good it was to get out of that hold – some of the lads that were sick never came out of the hold alive and the stench was just terrible".

"We left Borneo on the 10th July and after six nightmare days wondering if we would see the light of day again, we at last arrived at Manila on the 16th July where we stayed until the 9th August. It was a Godsend as we had time to barter for some food to supplement our very bad rice ration. We helped get our sick lads what food we could but as we sailed off on the 9th, we wondered what our fate would be. We stopped the next day at San Fernando, but were not allowed up top – then on the 12th we set off again. On the 13th, we ran into such a storm. We thought the sea was rough on our trip to Halifax Nova Scotia on our way to Singapore all those years before, but none of us had experienced anything like this. The whole ship was tossed out of the sea, we were thrown about like matchsticks. Many of our sick boys passed away that night while the American submarines took advantage of the storm and took action on our convoy. A lot of us managed to get up on deck and cling hold of a mast, and many of us even tied ourselves to the side of the ship. We could see many of the ships getting hit by torpedoes and go up in flames. The worst thing I saw was as these ships went down, our dear boys that had got on to a liferaft were just thrown off them by a Jap soldier – a thing they had promised us on the day we left Singapore. They were now to be shark bait. We all now thought this would be our end for the whole area was aflame with the burning oil from the ships that went down. I can still hear the screams of the men in the water – many of them were caught up in the flames and I would like to think that it was quick for them, but I fear from the sound of their screams that alas it was not. The whole sky was so bright that the American subs could see us as clear as they would have done if it had been daylight. I don't think they knew that we were on board and to them they were just Japanese ships waiting to be picked off, but by the end of the war we had lost as many men to this type of death as we did as prisoners of the Japs".

"The battle raged on into the next day, the 14th of August, and so did the storm, and the ship we were on took such a hammering it started to list heavily to one side. The boys still down in the hold stood no chance and those that did survive only did so by swimming out of the hold. I remember being up on deck with my mate, Sergeant Ager, holding on for dear life, and we were in water up to our waists so God knows how they survived in the hold. The waves were breaking right over the ship now and we feared it was to be burial at sea for us. I said to Sergeant Ager 'we are going to be shark bait, old mate'. He replied 'don't give up now, Percy. You hold on for dear life', which I did. We didn't even have the strength to talk as you can imagine how much you had to shout above the noise of the storm. I thought I would never see land again and after what seemed hours of holding on, the ship now having nearly rolled right onto its side, there was an almighty noise as we ran onto some rocks. We must have hit them hard as we went right up onto them with such an impact that men were just thrown overboard".

"Most of the Japs met their end like this as well as my dear comrades and for us that had survived it was nothing but a miracle. The ship stopped rolling now but the sea still came over at us, and I just kept holding on. I gripped so tightly that I lost all feeling in my hands and arms but after some hours the sea started to calm down and at last there was quiet. Those that had survived started to talk to one another again of how lucky they were. Many were asking if we had seen their friend but so many had gone flying by me into the sea that I had no idea who they had been".

"I think there were more of us left alive than there were Japs. We talked about taking over, but where could we go? There was no way of leaving the ship although we were only a few hundred yards offshore. The rocks were so large we knew we could not cross them and if we had tried to swim, we were in such a state that we would have been smashed up on the rocks. After a while we all started to get so hungry, but all the rice coppers had been washed over – the only food we could find was the burnt rice that had been scraped from the sides of the coppers. This had been stored in bags and although it was soaked with sea water, it was something to eat, even though it did give us bad stomach ache. We still thought this was it for us now, but then on the 16th, out of the blue, came a Jap destroyer – but of course they couldn't get near us. The Japs with us were all shouting and ranting on and they soon showed their old selves again in their true colours by pushing prisoners out of the way and over the side of the ship. The Jap destroyer ran out a small boat with a rope fixed to it and the Japs on our ship fixed the other end of this rope to our ship. The sea was still rising high and we had to wait until the boat rose up on the crest of each wave and then jump into the boat when it was at the highest point – needless to say, many men missed the boat and got washed away into the sea and rocks. For them.... once again they were shark bait. When it came for me to jump I could not even see the boat for I had lost my sight, owing to the lack of food and vitamins. My mate Sergeant Ager said 'don't worry Percy, I'm here with you mate. When I push you in the back, you just jump forward and you will make the boat'. This is what I did and I remember landing on top of all the other blokes. I don't think I hurt any of them too much, for they all looked after me until Sergeant Ager got into the boat. I owed him a lot at that time for he led me out of danger for some time. Once on board the Jap destroyer the Japanese sailors gave us the best bowl of rice that I had eaten for a long time. They were much kinder to us than the camp guards ever were. They took us to Formosa on the 17th of August where another ship was waiting to take us on to Japan, or at least this is what the Japanese sailors told us. Sergeant Ager said to me 'look at all those ships, old mate'. But look as I may, I still could not see. It was really worrying me as I feared I would never see again and I knew it would mean my death, for I had learnt enough to know that I would be no good to the Japs blind – I knew they would kill me and I think what scared me most about it was that I would not even see my killer. I thought to myself 'all you will feel Percy, is the bayonet go in and that

107

will be you done for'. That's why I know how much I owe Sergeant Ager for looking out for me at that time".

"We arrived in Japan on the 27th August 1944. I remember being pushed about all the time but my mate Sergeant Ager kept reassuring me that he was with me and that I was not to worry. We boarded a train much the same as we had been taken to Thailand on to build their damn railway. It was now the 28th of August and as we bumped along on the trip another miracle happened for me – my sight started to return. I gave thanks for that I can tell you. I looked all around me and even though the sights were only of my poor skeleton-like mates, it was a sight I thought I would never see again – it was just wonderful. We finally arrived at our camp, a place called Ube off Fukurka, and after the nightmare of the Japs counting us, we were put into a long hut. The hut had been divided into six rooms and they pushed as many of us as they could into these rooms. They then put a Sergeant in charge of each room, and thank God for once they never picked me, for every morning they would come and inspect the room and if it was not to their liking they would take it out on the Sergeant and give him a beating".

"The Japanese Commandant in charge of the camp only had one arm – he had lost the other one fighting in China. But if he hit you, it felt like you had been hit with a sledge hammer, he had so much strength in that one arm. If only he could have been as kind as my best mate Len Gilbey. I sat for a moment and wondered how Len was making out. Was he still alive without me to look out for him? I gave a silent prayer that he was still alive and well but I was soon brought back to reality when a Jap guard came shouting 'all men work'. We were mustered up and taken outside where we were told to strip off, which we did. We were then given a black shirt and a pair of shorts, also in black. One chap said, 'daft buggers. They won't see me in the dark now Percy, will they mate?" but we soon found out why they were black – we were marched off to work down a coal mine! We were given a lamp that clipped around our head and the Commandant said 'you men work hard, Japanese be good to you, you bring up much coal, you be alright'. With that we started down into the mine. I counted 1,002 steps and each one was over 18 inches high. We arrived down at the coal face which was about 4' high, so you can imagine how bent up we were. It was so hot the sweat was pumping out of us, and we had not even started work yet. One of the chaps said 'these bloody Japs. They make us build their damned railway, now they want us to provide the bloody coal for them to run the trains on'. No one answered him as a Jap shouted out 'you no talk, just work. You load three trucks, you then go up top'. There were 10 of us in this work party and we were meant to be the fittest men. We set to break-ing away the coal from the face which was such hard work. After a while we were all choking and spitting up coal dust and our eyes stung. It was terrible but we worked on as best we could until we got the three trucks full and thank God the Jap guard kept his word and let us up top. It was such hard work to climb up those 1,002 steps after being bent up work-ing for hours in the dark and during the time that I was working there, one of us always fell down through sheer exhaustion and one of the others would catch you and save you from falling to your death. Once on top and outside we just collapsed to the ground coughing and splut-tering up all the coal dust from our lungs and with my eyes now bad it took me some time before I could see properly so I would just lay there with my eyes shut. I think the Japs knew how hard we had to work and they just left us to lay there until the other shifts were finished, which sometimes was another couple of hours. We were then all rounded up and the nightmare of counting us would begin. I know today the Japs rule the world with their computers and technology but it surprises me, for in all my time as a prisoner, they could never count us. Once they had us counted we were marched back to camp; they would try and get us to do the goose step but it was all we could do to walk, so none of us would do it. They beat a few of us to try and get us to do it but they soon lost interest. I think most of the Japs wanted to get back to camp as much as we did, for they had been in the mine with us and knew what it was like".

"After about three months of this hard work, we were all so very sick but if you did not go down the mine and work they stopped your rice ration. Those who were sick and unable to work, received very little food, since those of us that were working only received a pittance of rice, and we needed as much of that as possible to keep us going. Then one day the Japs said they were picking men to work in a new tunnel and they picked out three parties of us with about 10 in each. I was put in charge of one party, Sergeant Ager another, and Sergeant Dale (who was in the Beds and Herts Regiment) was given charge of the other. There was one Jap with each party and I think once again my life was saved by sheer luck for the Jap over our party was to turn out to be the best Jap I have ever met – his name was Morrison and he was such a steady old boy and he was not too bad to me at all. We were told this new tunnel would allow 3,000,000 tonnes of coal to be brought up and our job was to make a 1m wide x 1m deep drainage system. We then had to put up shuttering then mix concrete and ballast and cast this to form the new drain. I soon found how lucky I was to have this particular Jap with us, for he was tall for a Jap and therefore never hit out at me because I was tall. The chaps in the other two parties had a small Jap in charge of them and they took great delight in beating their prisoners. I soon told the lads with me that 'we are lucky to have this Morrison over us. He works with us and is steady. If we work along with him I feel sure he will be fair to us'. The lads agreed with me and so we tried to do our best for him and it paid off. He made sure we had proper breaks and lots of drink which I know saved a lot of us. One morning he said to me 'I have big machine coming to break up rocks to make ballast for concrete' – up to now we had been doing it with just our sledge hammers – what a Godsend it was. He told me 'I put you in charge of machine'. I had to load it with large rocks, and it would break them up into small pieces, about 2" etc., and I then mixed it with cement, all by hand of course, on a large iron plate, then the lads took it and poured it into the shuttering. When we took the shuttering away, if there were any holes we quickly filled them in with cement before the Japs inspected it. The only trouble with the rock breaker was that it was so noisy so now, as well as not being able to see very well, the noise had started to make me deaf – but I was still alive".

"One day the Japs asked for bricklayers and as I could not hear what they were saying a Welsh chap called Danny Morris stuck my hand up with his and shouted out 'we're bricklayers'. He said 'come on Sarge, follow me'. I thought 'what the hell has he got me into now?' The Jap gave Danny a blueprint drawing and said 'you build this?' Once again Danny said 'yes we can build anything'. I managed to hear the word 'build' and I looked at Danny to see him just smile at me and say 'don't look so worried, Sarge. I'm saving your bloody life, old mate'. I shouted out 'what you saying?' He just shouted back 'don't worry, I'll tell you later' for the rock crusher was still bellowing out and I just didn't know what was going on. I followed on behind Danny and the Jap Engineer. Danny was also a Sergeant and was one of the bravest Welsh men I have ever met. He had certainly put our lives on the line this time, but nothing worried him and once we got to the part of the mine where we were to carry out our bricklaying, the Jap showed us where we were to build, showed us where the bricks, sand and cement were and then went off and left us to it. Danny looked at me and said 'just listen'. I couldn't hear a thing now and said to him, 'Danny, I can't hear a damn thing'. He replied 'nor can I old mate. It's just so nice and quiet here'. I could hear all that Danny had said and I smiled at him and said 'Danny, I can hear you – I can bloody well hear you. I'm not deaf any more'. He looked at me and said 'no, you daft bugger, but you would have been if I ain't stuck your bloody hand up and saved you from that damn machine. That's what was making you deaf, you silly old fool – and all that hard work will kill you'. I replied 'yes Danny, but I'm no bricklayer' to which he laughed and said 'no, nor am I, but we can manage this old mate – it's so bloody dark down here who's gonna see it anyway?' We set to and started our new career as bricklayers; we could see from the drawing that we had to build a square of bricks and at a certain height, we had to leave a couple of bricks out at either side for a rope to pass through which they pulled the trucks along with. After a while we soon got the hang of it and once built, we had to put a concrete floor in the bottom. Once we finished the building the Japs soon put an engine in it and this would pull the trucks along. One day while we were building one of these, I lost Danny and when he did return he said 'you watch when the next lot of trucks come by, and keep well out of the way of them'. I said 'what the hell have you been up to now?' 'You'll see,' he said. It was not long before the trucks came by and as they got by us the wheels of two of the trucks came flying off and there was an almighty clatter as coal and trucks flew everywhere. I looked at Danny, who had a broad smile right across his face, and said 'you've done it now old son – that's us done for now.' He said 'you just make out you're deaf, I'll soon sort 'em out if they start on us boyo'. The place was soon overflowing with Japs shouting and ranting on at the top of their voices; it soon came for our turn to be questioned by them and my heart was in my mouth. Danny said 'remember you're deaf, leave this to me.' I told him 'yeah, that's what I'm worried about, but anyway it's been nice knowing you mate'. As we came before the Jap Commandant, who was in one hell of a rage, I thought 'best of luck Danny old boy – get us out of this one if you can.' The Jap shook his one arm at us with his pickle stick held firmly in his hand and hit us both across the face, then shouted out 'you men know who sabotage trucks?' I kept quiet and Danny said 'my friend and I know nothing, sir. We are bricklayers for Japanese; we too busy to look at trucks'. As the Jap walked to me he must have seen the sweat pumping out of me and my heart was pumping so fast I thought it was going to explode. He looked up at me. I kept my head bowed and he said 'you, where you work?' Before I could answer, Danny spoke up 'he can't hear you sir, he is deaf', and pointed to his ears. 'He works with me, we are bricklayers. We work long way from trucks'. The Jap walked back to Danny and looked him right in the eye, then walked right round him and came back right in front of him. He gave a big sigh and said 'you bricklayers, you go work hard'. We quickly turned and went. I remember saying, once we got well away from the Japs, 'Danny, don't you ever

111

do that again – I don't think my heart can stand it'. He just laughed and said 'got to keep em on their toes you know' ".

"We were given a piece of radish to eat with our rice now as many of us still had dysentery. 'Radish good for you' they told us, but I found something else that helped the dysentery. The Japs paid us a little for our hard work, and when I got the chance to buy any extras to help me, I did. One such thing was a tin of white powder meant for cleaning your teeth, but I soon found that a spoonful of it sprinkled over your rice helped stop your dysentery – I suppose it was because it was like chalk".

"One day as we returned to camp we found a lot of the men were digging a large trench around the camp. We wondered why they were building a moat around us and many rumours started to spread around the camp but then one morning we were all paraded in front of the Commandant and he informed us 'you are wondering why you dig trench. I tell you. If Americans invade, this trench be your grave. You all be killed'. We knew now things could not be going too well for them and although it pleased us, the fear of being killed and having to look at your grave every day was just not good. One of the Japanese working in the mine had come from America before the war and had not been allowed to return, and from him we received little bits of news how things were going. He told us 'Americans bombing Japan now', but he just did not dare tell us too much".

"The Japs started telling us we might get Red Cross parcels but none of us believed them – for all these years we had received nothing. A few days later they brought some of the parcels out of one of the mines. They gave us one parcel to share between four of us. One of the guards was watching us so much that our Medical Officer said 'I'm go-ing to bribe him and give him a few things from the parcel' – he gave him a piece of cheese. The Jap actually smiled at him and thanked him and quickly went off. Later that day he came up to our MO and started hitting him and was shouting at him 'this no good, it no lather' – he had obviously thought it was a bar of soap. I think our MO soon learnt not to give them anything else".

"The food was now very bad and we put it down to the Americans now bombing Japan and disrupting the food supplies. The Japs brought in some whale meat which was cut into 2" squares and cooked for us but you dare not swallow it for it was just like eating chewing gum – it just lasted and lasted so we just chewed it for as long as we could then spat it out. They also gave us what they called gravy but it tasted more like waste engine oil. We were working the mines full time now in shifts. One day when I was finishing a day shift, we met the lads waiting to go down on the night shift. We said to them 'anything better for dinner today?' to which they replied 'brown dog'. There had been this very large brown dog around the camp for the last few days and the Japs said to the cook house 'if you can catch it, you can have it'. They knew how bad our food was so they caught the dog and cooked it up. The meat of the dog went to the lads in the sick hut and we had just a little of the gravy that they had made from the bones etc. It was just like a few beads of fat floating in hot water but no one said anything for now it was that or nothing. The chap who had cooked the dog was given the name of 'Brown Dog' and is still called it to this day whenever we meet. For the next couple of days we received no food, then on the third day the Japs brought us a lot of small crabs to eat. Our MO said 'just break the claws off and then eat the lot' which we did, shell and all – he told us it would give us calcium. The next day we just received oranges which we roasted until they were black then ate the lot, skin and all. What a state we were in as the juice ran down our faces – but it was something to eat and we were so hungry now".

"I had now got cement poisoning and the skin was just falling off my hands – it made me feel terrible and was to be something that I was to suffer from for years to come. I was so run down now that I got a large boil on my backside and so I was put in the sick hut. The doctor was a Russian chap named Patroski who told me 'you must lay down on your bed face down and hold tight on to the bed – I'll have to lance it for you'. There was no anaesthetic and I thought over the last few years that I had learnt all there was to know about pain but this was the worst. I bit on my rice sack so hard I bit right through it in seconds. It did the trick though and he got the poison out. My mate Sergeant Ager, who stood watching, said to me 'I thought you were going to break the bed you were gripping it so tightly'. Then he laughed and said 'you must be hungry old mate. Look, you've tried to eat your rice sack'. I said 'I could eat a horse I'm so hungry – if we don't get better food soon, none of us will be left alive'. I was given the job of working in the Japs' garden for a week until I felt a bit better. I was not able to pinch anything though, as they watched you like a hawk, but the fresh air did me good after being down the mine in all that dust. After a while I felt I could breathe much better, but I was coughing up soot for days".

"After a week I was back down the mine, but we were all so hungry we had very little strength to work. That evening we took an air raid from the Americans and we feared this would be our end, but while the Japs made for the shelters, I and some of the others went and raided the Japs' garden. We took potato tops, put them in a tin and cooked them under a steam pipe that came out of one of the buildings. Just to have something to eat was so good, and to us those potato tops tasted so good they might just as well have been spring cabbage".

"Nothing was said to us now by the Japs but the next day I was down the mine when we were all told to come up top. Once we had all gathered on top, the Jap guard said 'all men back to camp'. We feared we were now to be shot, but as we marched into camp, we were met by a new lot of Japanese soldiers – our one armed Commandant had gone. The new Jap Officer said 'men, war now over, war finished''. Well, we didn't know whether to laugh or cry. We fell to our knees. Some men were crying, others were hugging one another. Was it really true, or was this just another Japanese ploy? Were they just playing a sick game with us? The trench around the camp was still there, so many thoughts went through my mind. At that moment I saw my dear Joyce.... my parents.... my sister.... – was I *really* going home to be with them at last? While we were left locked in our thoughts, the Japs vanished. Then within hours, American planes came flying over. They circled round and then out came the parachutes dropping us fresh food and clothes. Many of these fell in the sea and we swam out to get them, strengthened by the sheer excitement of it all. On the end of the parachutes were 50 gallon oil drums. Some of the parachutes did not open and the drums crashed through the roofs of nearby houses, but who cared? We were now free and at last had food to eat".

"We soon kitted ourselves out and had some of the food – the best we had eaten for three and a half years. Boy, did it taste good! But then, alas, one of our lads died; he had been very ill and I think the excitement of it all was just too much for him to take. He was Leslie Howard from Heacham in Norfolk. It was the day after we had been set free, and, like all the other poor lads that had died before him, was a smashing bloke just trying to do his best to stay alive, but like him, many more were to die from the treatment that they had received over those three and a half years of hell, before they were to leave Japan".

"We found a tin of paint and in big bold letters we wrote the word 'thanks' on the roof of one of the huts for the Americans to see how grateful we were to them. It was well into the middle of August 1945 now and one morning Danny Morris said 'let's sew our stripes on and go out for a walk' which we did, and Sergeant Ager and W. Spencer joined us. We met many of the local Japs who all bowed their heads to us. Boy, did we play on that! We had suffered our fair share of bowing to Japs over that last three and a half years, and we felt it only right that they kept bowing down to us. We met one Jap and asked him 'you have beer?' He went off and soon returned with a half pint bottle for us to share. We tried to drink it but it made us all sick, for we were still in such a bad way. It soon made our heads spin and we started giggling, but who cared – we were free at last. It was such a good feeling, and as we walked back to camp we spoke to one another of how lucky we all were to have come through it all".

"Americans soon arrived and we were given orders that we were to make ready to move off. As we left Ube, it felt as we had left a part of our lives there in those mines and it still feels the same these 50 years on. We boarded a train that took us to Wakeyma and for the first time we were able to sit in a proper carriage – it really was so good after all the cattle trucks we had been in over the years. We left Ube on the 13th September 1945 and arrived at Wakeyma on the 15th where we boarded the American ship, Consation, where we were debugged and given a good medical. I was given some treatment for my cement poisoning which helped a lot and it was so good to be clean at last after looking like black skeletons for so long. We now started to feel like men again. The food was so very good but after not being used to food I soon got bloated. On the 17th September there was a terrible storm so we could not depart but the next day we set off for Okinawa where we arrived on the 20th September. Here we boarded the American ship, Huskel. We

Welcome!

British Columbia meets you with a cordial welcome, and a deep appreciation of your sacrifice in defense of all that free men cherish and hold dear.

We who were spared the actual physical impact of war give thanks, humbly and gratefully, for all the safety and security which we enjoyed in those years when you, and whole peoples, endured with grim patience the heel of the aggressor.

You have come up out of the Valley of the Shadow of Death, to be with friends whose warm good wishes will follow you wherever you go. May Good Fortune attend you, and may you find the contentment in which to rebuild your lives and to go on, in the peace and happiness which you have done so much to win for yourselves and for us all.

The Government of the Province of
British Columbia

Victoria, British Columbia, Canada

set off again on the 22nd of September – it was a lovely trip and when we arrived at Manila on the 25th September we all started to feel that much better. The better food and drink we were now receiving was at last starting to take effect on us and we felt that bit stronger. We all said 'thank God. At least by the time we get home we should look OK'. My eyesight was now a lot better and the medical boys assured me that with proper food and rest I would be OK. We had a wonderful time at Manila. Lady Mountbatten came to visit us and welcomed us back to freedom at last. She was so very nice to us, and it was so good to see one of our own beautiful women again. We were given plenty of beer and cigars – the Americans really did us proud. After a while here we were told we were to get ready to move off again, this time on board an American aircraft carrier. On the 9th October 1945 we set sail again, and once more the food and care was just excellent. We took plenty of walks around the flight deck and many of the lads would say 'I can walk further around this ship than I could around my village back home', the carrier was just so big. Everyone was talking of home now because at last we really allowed ourselves to believe we were going to finally see home again. I used to shed a tear every time I thought of it. We had film shows on board and one day as we sat watching a film, at the end of it an American voice came over the air waves and said 'gentlemen, we shall be arriving at Honolulu in a short time and hope you will all enjoy yourselves'. Well, it was like a dream come true for us, for none of us ever dreamed we would ever get to stay in Honolulu. Most of us were just country boys who had not been to the next county, yet here we were in some of the best places in the world. We had to keep pinching ourselves to prove that we were not still dreaming. We arrived at Honolulu on 20th October 1945 and although we only stayed one day here, it will be a day I shall never forget. One could spend a lifetime just relaxing in Honolulu!"

"We set sail again, this time for Victoria, Canada. Boy, what a welcome they gave us here. As we came in to harbour there were bands playing and all the other ships were sounding their hooters and firing jets of water up into the air. It was such a wonderful sight – most of us had tears just running down our faces for we were still emotionally drained and it was a sight that none of us thought we would ever see again. We were told to get ourselves ready to leave ship and they informed us that the people of Canada were there to meet us and that we would be going home with them for a holiday. I departed that great big ship with my dear mate, John Ager, a man I owed so much to, for he had looked after me so much through those nightmare times".

"I said 'come on old son, I'll look after you now.' He replied 'get away with you. I've looked after you this far, I'm not stopping now'. We left that ship feeling so happy and as we came down onto the dockside, we were met by a Mr and Mrs Vickery. They embraced us as if we were their own sons. They were so wonderful to us. They told us 'you will be coming home with us now boys – we will soon have you looking just fine'. Mr Vickery said 'once you start eating mother's cooking, you will certainly grow and don't worry, she will soon let those trousers out for you, so you just eat and eat and be happy with us'. They told us that they had been brought up in England – Mrs Vickery in Scotland and Mr Vickery in Cumbria. They had three children – two boys and one girl. It was now the 26th of October 1945 and as we arrived at the Vickerys' home we knew we were going to be happy with them. It was a wonderful homestead and we were soon playing tennis with the children and eating such wonderful dishes that Mrs Vickery cooked for us. Mr Vickery took us shooting and salmon fishing; he took us to the Indian settlements to see how they lived – such wonderful totem poles! The scenery of the country was just breathtaking. They say 'God works in mysterious ways, his wonders to perform', and after what we had been through, he at last brought us to people who showed us nothing but love and care for their fellow humans, so unlike the Japs".

"When the day came to say goodbye we were all in tears and I think it fair to say they were going to miss us as much as we would miss them. Mr Vickery drove us to the docks to board our ship but when we got there we found out we were to travel by train to New York – yes, the Big Apple. We said our final farewell to Mr Vickery who told us 'I'm sure going to miss you boys, but thanks for what you have given and suffered for us to remain free. One day the world will know just what heroes you have all been'. We moved towards him and took it in turns to embrace him for he had been like a real father to us over those two weeks. I said to him 'you know we can never repay you for your kindness towards us and we shall remember you for the rest of our lives' to which he replied 'don't you thank me old son, it is I that owe you so much'. As we boarded the train we felt sad to be leaving but the thought of our loved ones waiting for us was what had kept us going all this time and we knew it would not be long before we would see them again now that every day was bringing us nearer to them. We waved to Mr Vickery until we were completely out of sight and then sat back and spoke to all the other lads who assured us they had been just as well looked after by their hosts".

"We had a great journey to New York and at every station we stopped at people met us with baskets of food, beer and cigars so someone must have told them we were coming through. We left Canada on the 6th November 1945 and arrived in New York on the 11th November to board the great Queen Mary – what a ship, the best of them all. We felt like royalty now – you name it they had it on board, even shops. We rested up and just enjoyed being alive. Most of us still bore the effects of our prisoner of war camps and we knew in our hearts that however long we lived, we could never heal the scars from those three and a half years of hell but thanks to the good people of Canada and now our trip on the Queen Mary, our lives were improving day by day".

"We arrived back in Southampton, England on the 18th November 1945 to a very cold, foggy day. There was no one to greet us this time and as we left that great ship and set foot on our dear home land again, it was just too much for most of us. I think even the hardest man shed a tear that day as it was our dream come true. We thought of all our dear friends that had not made it back and I think most of us knew just how lucky we were to have come through it all. We were then taken to a transit camp where we stayed for a few days to be given medicals and then our demob suits were handed out with our rail passes. We all said our goodbyes to our mates who were heading to different parts of the country and all promised to keep in touch, for we alone were the ones that really knew what it had been like and we knew in our hearts we had to keep alive the spirit that had kept us going and had bound us together as one. Those of us bound for Cambridgeshire boarded our train and settled back to enjoy the trip. It was very cold for us after the heat we had endured in the tropics, although it had been cold in Japan. We really were starting to feel it now and most of the lads said 'yeah, we are back in good old England again. I hope my old girls covered the sprouts over to keep the frost off them'. We would all laugh and say 'you daft bugger you – who cares if the sprouts get frozen as long as we are home?' But he replied 'yes, but I like me sprouts and they are no good once they get too much frost'. Another chap replied 'daft bugger. They're a lot better after a frost'. As I sat listening to this conversation I thought to myself how good it was to hear. We had been away all these years and now the lads were talking just like good old country boys again, worried about their vegetables being frozen. Yes, we were home alright and as the train pulled into Littleport station there waiting for me was my dear mother and father. You can imagine the scene – just so emotional".

"After hugging the life out of them, I said 'where's Joyce?' 'Don't worry lad' came dad's reply, 'she's a waiting for yer at home'. Our friend, Joe Godbold, had brought them to meet me and as we drove home to Little Ouse to the Anchor Inn that I knew as home, mother said 'I was going to the doctors tonight son, but I shall leave it now for I feel that having you home is better than any tonic he can give me'. As we arrived at the Anchor Inn my heart was in my mouth and pumping so fast it felt as it would explode in my chest – it was a feeling I had felt many times at the hands of my captors but this time it was through a mixture of sheer emotion and excitement at seeing Joyce again. Yes, after four years apart we were back together. I can't tell you enough how my love for her had carried me through those dark days and to be with her once again was a dream come true. Once again I shall leave you all to your imaginations to imagine the scenes at the Anchor Inn that night....".

"It was now December 1945 and I spent time visiting old friends and the parents and sweethearts of those dear friends that had not come home. I don't think at the time I could tell them just how bad it had been or how cruel a death their loved one had suffered, only to tell them how proud they could be of him. After Christmas 1945 I knew I had to do something or go mad – my mind kept taking me back to my time as a prisoner and one day Joe Godbold said to me 'Percy, if you want to come and work for me on the farm you know you can. You can come and go as you like, just give yourself time to settle in'. Joe was foreman at Headings Farm which was just down the road. He told me 'I've got a lot of horses that need breaking'. As you know, I always loved horses and so I said yes. I soon found myself going full time as I wanted to save as much money as I could so that Joyce and I could get married at Easter, as we had planned to. I worked hard and saved hard and that Easter, April 1946, I married my darling Joyce. Oh how I dreamed of this day".

"A few weeks before the wedding, I gave Joyce a present that I had brought home from Japan for her – one of the silk parachutes that the Americans had dropped our supplies into our prison camp with. Joyce made a slip out of it to wear on our wedding day. You know how they say have something old, something new, something borrowed and something blue – well we had borrowed the parachute and to this day it is a very special item in our lives. After the wedding we moved in with Joyce's parents at the White Horse farm where her father was foreman for Luddington Farms at Little Ouse Road. It was not long before a council house came up in Little Ouse so I went to see the Council and they said 'yes, you can have it for eight shillings a week', which I agreed to and so we moved into our first real home together".

"I was now working on piece work so there was good money to be earned and being out in the fresh air was doing me good, even if I did get tired quickly. I used to tell myself how lucky I was and on those days

119

when I would say this to myself you can bet that that night I would have a bad nightmare. Poor Joyce must have been scared out of her life but over the years she has learnt to live with them and thanks to her love and care I am here today to tell you the story. My father had a lot of empty sheds at the Anchor Inn so I started to keep show rabbits in them, which I exhibited at Ely, Littleport and Feltwell. I won many prizes with them. The rabbits that I did not think were up to showing I took to Ely market, which made me a few extra shillings. One day while I was at Ely market I had done so well and made a good bit, that when the pigs came on sale I bid for a sow and got her – this was just the start and I soon went on to breed pigs. The farm where I worked allowed me so much bran for the rabbits that I was able to mix it up for the pigs as well, and I also got all the waste carrots, parsnips and potatoes. I got an old boiling copper and used to boil it all up for the pigs. The first day I did this it really upset me, for it took my mind back to those bloody death camps and although the food was only for the pigs, I could see that it was 90% better than we had been given while prisoners. It all came rushing back to me and I stood on my own with tears running down my face. I said to myself 'pull yourself together Percy', but it had really got hold of me. I think I had been telling myself that I was alright when really, like most of us, my nerves were shot. After a while it passed and as I fed the pigs, I told them, 'you don't know how lucky you are' and that they were fed much better than I and my mates had been. I thought more of them than I did the Japs, and when the day came to take two of them to market, fattened and ready, I felt really bad. But I needed the money and so had to be hard".

"In the summer of 1946 I was hit with a recurrence of malaria, which really knocked me back. *I* knew what it was, but the doctors didn't and for the next twenty years, every June, it would come back to me, so it wasn't just my mind that wouldn't let me forget those nightmare times – even that damned malaria still had me in its grasp. You know by now how wonderful all FEPOWS' wives are, and without the love and care from my dear Joyce, I would not have made it this far. One day, soon after this first attack, I was at Ely market when I saw one of my fellow prisoners. He asked me how I was and I told him all that I was doing. He looked at me and said 'you're lucky, I just can't work anymore. I live in fear all the time and I burst out crying at the least little thing. I'm finished mate – I know I can't go on much longer like this. No one understands what we've been through, do they?" I felt so sorry for him and it made me realise how lucky I was to have my dear Joyce and also how right I had been to put myself into my work to keep my mind occupied. I also knew that it was the only way I was going to get on in life. I told myself that if I could work nearly 18 hours a day for three and a half years for the Japs on just six ounces of rice a day, then I can certainly work hard for myself and Joyce to give us a good life together – and I would like to think this is what we have done together".

"1947 came and with it came the floods. The banks of the river burst and flooded Feltwell Fen. The corn stacks all had to be moved and we waded our way over Little Ouse bridge on to Mortons Farm to build up new stacks. After weeks of carting stuff from Headings Farm over to Mortons Farm we worked all the hours God sent and we were all dead on our feet but once it was all done that was it, work finished, owing to the floods. I thought 'thank God I've got my rabbits and pigs to help me get by' but we soon heard that Thomsons Farm wanted men to dig dykes and so my father and I went along with Mr H Cole and Mr W Murfitt and offered our services. It was really hard work and once again it brought back to me how the Japs had made us build that dyke around our camp. One day I was quite done in, and my father said 'are you alright, old son?' I told him about the time the Japs had told us that the dyke around the camp was to be our grave. He gripped my arm and said 'son, I know what it must be like for you – why not call it a day' but I told him 'no dad, I'm alright now I'm with you' and we just smiled at one another and got stuck into it – we both knew what we meant to one another".

"By the end of the spring the land had dried out and we were able to get back on the land again, but by now another miracle had happened for me – my darling Joyce was expecting our first child. I had heard so many of the chaps as prisoners talk about their children, and that of course was something I dreamed of having one day, and now that day had come. My darling Joyce presented me with our dear daughter on the 2nd May 1947 and we named her Kathleen. She brought so much light into my life and took away some of the pain that I had suffered. I felt so lucky I now had two beautiful women to love and care for – it was like having a new life. Oh how happy I was!"

"The year soon went by as we were so busy, what with all the rabbits and pigs to look after, and our new baby. It was such a smashing time, it was just so good to be alive. I was so very lucky – after all I had been through I felt on top of the world but I often sat and thought about all my dear mates that had not come back; they were never to hold their own child or have a home life. I would sit and think back to all that jungle that I had cut back to make a cemetery and to this day I can still see the faces of those dear lads as I lay them to rest and I still have the nightmares of my mates sitting up and looking at me as I cremated their poor twisted bodies. Joyce would say 'come back Percy, don't sit and think about the past. You're OK now, you're here with us, all your loved ones'. I would smile at her and say 'yes love, I know how lucky I am, I'm one of the lucky ones".

"1948 soon came and I still had plenty of work and Joyce was kept busy feeding the pigs and the rabbits for me, as well as caring for our dear daughter. We also had a good garden in which we grew all our own food. We worked hard together and things were going well for us. I remember saying to Joyce how happy I was as we sat chatting one evening and she said 'you'll have to keep working hard Percy lad – I am expecting again'. I didn't mind working hard – compared to those three and a half years of hell, anything was heaven. I was so happy to learn that she was expecting again, and on the 6th of June 1948 she presented me with a son – my family was complete now. I don't think anyone could have been happier than me; I called my son Michael and I don't think I could ever thank God enough for the happiness that he and Kathleen have brought me. I have always been so proud of them and Joyce and I must have done something right, as they have never been a bit of trouble to us and we are as proud of them today as we were that first time we ever held them in our arms. They and Joyce gave me back my life".

"When 1949 arrived I was so busy with my own livestock that I decided to work for myself. I noticed that there was 20 acres of land for hire or sale from the Church, so I wrote to the Bishop of Ely. I also wrote to the Council about a holding and they offered me a holding of 35 acres at Fences Farm, Stowbridge. I kept writing to the Church Council about the land they had for sale but they kept me waiting about so long that I took the holding. I wrote to the Bishop and told him that I had lost interest in buying their land as they were so slow in letting me know. I took all my rabbits and young pigs to Ely market and sold them all. I spoke to Joe Godbold who wished me all the best and told me if I needed any help at all I was just to give him a call – 'that's what friends are for' he said. I bought a little old autocycle – you may remember them, like a bicycle with an engine in the back wheel. As I couldn't do much on my own farm until the spring, I was glad of Joe's offer, and I carried on working for him, and thanks to my old autocycle I was able to get to his farm without walking. As the good people of the fens will know, in those days we had to walk everywhere – not like today, when you just jump in the car. Looking back, they were such happy days and I was one of the real lucky ones for my dear Joyce worked as hard as me, if not harder. When we worked on the land the children would play beside us and as they got older, they helped us as well".

"How lucky I have been – I've had a good life, apart from those four years of hell away from my homeland, but of all my life it is those four years that always haunt me. I know they will never leave me until the day I die and then I hope I shall again meet all those dear lads who gave their lives for our today".

Thank you, Percy, for sharing your story with us. I feel sure the readers feel as privileged to read it as I am at being given the honour of writing it for you. My hope is that people will learn from it and never allow such horrific things to ever happen again, for good must win over evil or else we are all finished.

God bless you and your family, Percy. I wish you long life and happiness and thank you for my today.

Footnote:

The one-armed Japanese Commandant was found by the Americans in 1945 and was later hung for his war crimes.

Today Percy and Joyce are enjoying their retirement and live in their bungalow at Downham Market. Their children are not too far from them and Michael, Percy's son, farms 85 acres, so he must have enjoyed growing up on the farm helping dad – or is it in the blood, I hear you say. Percy told me that Michael's wife works hard to help him, just like Joyce has done over the years with Percy. Their daughter lives in Hunstanton with her family but Percy told me with a smile how she was a trained hairdresser and he still looks forward to her cutting his hair. They have four grandchildren. I could see how proud they were of them all by the way they spoke of them. I feel sure they won't need me to tell them how lucky they are to have a grandfather like Percy, for like me, they will know that our world today could do with more men like Percy. He has not been too well at the time of writing this story, but each day he gets a little stronger and this has been the first year since the end of the war that he has not been able to help get the harvest in. I am sure, like me, you will wish him a full recovery and let's hope he brings in many more harvests for many years to come.

Percy still has the spoon that fed him his rice in those nightmare days and, yes, to this day he still eats his meals with it – a thing he promised himself he would do until the day he dies. He still has his old razor too, although the threads are going on it now but he still says it gives him a good shave now that he has blades for it. These material things remind him every day of that time in his life, but I know how precious they are to him and long may he be around to keep using them.

Dear friends, before we start the letters section of the book, I would like to share with you over the next few pages, the order of service that those who were fit enough to attend took part in at Changi in 1945 to remember and say farewell to their friends and comrades who had not made it through those last four years. Many of you may have even been there, and also I know that many of you will have attended V.J. Day services here, this August 1995, to mark the 50th Anniversary of the end of the war and will have followed this service.

I would like to thank my dear friend Bert Grimes and his wife Rotha for forwarding the details to me. Many of you may remember my hero Bert from his true story in my last book "Forgotten Heroes" – also my friend and hero Robert Driver from that book. Well Robert and his dear wife Doris went back to the Far East to commemorate the 50th Anniversary and they have told me how very moving it was for them – it was a thing that Robert would never have believed that he would be able to do as he left the Far East those 50 years ago and he says "I have been so very lucky". But as you know, every FEPOW that came home always says "I was one of the lucky ones". It is a saying I hear so much from them that I nearly called this book "I was one of the lucky ones". I would just like to say, chaps, that *we* are the lucky ones – me and my generation. For so far we have been spared the hatred of world war – thanks to you brave men and to the suffering and sacrifice that you and your comrades gave for our today. And for that, I thank you with all my heart.

I know that as you look around you at our world today, you must sometimes wonder "was it worth it?", when you read in your newspapers that another dear old age pensioner has been mugged or murdered in their own home. All I can promise you all is that I shall always do my best to honour your dear departed comrades and to work hard to get the young people of today to show you the respect that you all deserve. On this note I am pleased to say that many of the school libraries have taken the books, so as I always say, you have marked the paths of history and your written word will go on to show the world what you gave to save all that is good – long after we are all dead and gone.

So many of you took the time to write to me or 'phone me to say how much you enjoyed reading the letters section in "Forgotten Heroes", that I have included some more of your letters that tell us all how that nightmare time is still affecting our lives today.

To all our dear FEPOW widows, my wife and I send our love and best wishes and please remember – don't suffer on your own. Contact your local FEPOW club branch and allow them to help you, for together we are one and we can help one another to enjoy life much better.

Final Thanksgiving Service

On the morning of Saturday August 11th 1945, as soon as the news came through that the Emperor of Japan had asked for terms, the ACG interviewed the Representative Officer with reference to a Thanksgiving Service. It was agreed to hold one as soon as the IJA passed on the news officially.

By Sunday August 19th, certain information having been volunteered by the IJA, it seemed reasonable to put on individual Church Thanksgiving Services that day, but to postpone the main service until later, when the National Anthem could be sung for the first time for many months, and meeting in a large body could be facilitated without the danger of provoking any of the guards into action.

A choir comprising members of all churches was massed, and a form of service drawn up, each denomination contributing. The service was, of necessity, short, on account of the inability of men to stand for any length of time.

A string orchestra, which had played once a month in St George's Church, and a harmonium, played by Lieutenant-Colonel Withers-Payne, led the service.

A bugler was present to play 'Last Post' and 'Reveille'. Except for funeral parties, no buglers had functioned in the camp for two years. Only Japanese bugle calls had been allowed.

On Saturday 26th August, it was decided to hold the service on the following day, on the Hospital square, this being less distance to walk than the Padang.

The Royal Engineers constructed a platform sixteen feet by eight feet, which was draped with the flags of the Allies, British, American and Dutch.

It had rained earlier, but this had cleared and the Sunday evening was fine though cloudy.

The crowds began to flock in from all areas by 1900hrs. Officers, bringing their own stools, were marshalled behind the altar – all others were marshalled with the Other Ranks. The sixteen most Senior Officers of Services and Nationalities were seated in front of the Altar.

By 1945 hrs it was conservatively estimated that 4,000 were present. Many hospital patients who were unable to leave their wards stood around the doors of their huts and joined in the singing.

All chaplains (less one Roman Catholic and one Dutch – who were sick), sixteen in number, assembled in St Andrew's vestry and then moved off to the square at 1945 hrs.

It was a service which will be long remembered. The vast body of men singing the hymns, the dull thunder of 4,000 voices and more saying the Lord's Prayer together formed a most fitting 'Nunc Dimittis' to the work of the churches in captivity. It was a spectacle of unity in Church and international relations commented upon and appreciated by all.

Holy Communion was celebrated at each of the Anglican churches at the conclusion of the Thanksgiving Service.

ORDER OF SERVICE
(27th August 1945)

Opening Sentences

HYMN: O God our help in ages past

Scriptural Reading: Jeremiah 29: 11-14 inclusive
Read in English by S/Chaplain M K Jones AIF
Read in Dutch by S/Chaplain J Van Wych Jurriance RNF

HYMN: Now thank we all our God

Prayers: Rev S W Barrett (M)AIF

ONE MINUTES SILENCE IN MEMORY OF OUR DEAD

LAST POST

"They shall grow not old......" etc – ACG

REVEILLE

HYMN: Praise my soul the King of Heaven

ADDRESS: Rev J N Lewis-Bryan ACG

HYMN: Abide with me

BENEDICTION

National Anthems:
United States of America
Holland
Great Britain

DEPART

126

ORDER OF SERVICE
(27th August 1995)

Opening Sentences

HYMN: O God our help in ages past

Scriptural Reading: Jeremiah 29: 11-14 inclusive

HYMN: Now thank we all our God

PRAYERS

ONE MINUTES SILENCE IN MEMORY OF OUR DEAD

LAST POST

"They shall grow not old......" etc.

RESPONSE

REVEILLE

HYMN: Praise, my soul, the King of Heaven...

ADDRESS: V B Jones CRC (Reading Rev J N Lewis-Bryan's Address)

HYMN: Abide with me; fast falls the eventide
(That wonderful Hymn my dear father sang over those poor victims, of the executioner.)

BENEDICTION

National Anthem

PROCESSION TO WAR MEMORIAL

LAST POST

TWO MINUTES SILENCE IN MEMORY OF OUR DEAD

FAR EAST PRISONER OF WAR PRAYER

RESPONSE

REVEILLE

BENEDICTION

DEPART

127

ADDRESS – by Rev J N Lewis-Bryan ACG

For three and a half years we have waited for this hour – the hour when we could all meet in heartfelt thankfulness to Almighty God for our safe deliverance.

We felt that it was only meet and right that we, who have borne the burden of these years together, should meet at the end in one great united service, in addition to those already held in churches of all denominations.

And so we are all here tonight.

There is an old proverb known to us all – Hope deferred maketh the heart sick, – but has it not been the star of hope shining undimmed through the long darkness of our night of captivity, which has led us on unswervingly in trust and confidence to the dawn of our liberation?

How long and how dark that night has been is known to us all to a greater or lesser degree. Those who have survived the horrors of the working camps in Thailand will have the memory of them seared for ever into their lives.

For all of us there has been the misery and wretchedness, the privations and the sufferings, the awful boredom and frustration - a sense of the wasted years - starvation and disease - and Death the Grim Reaper for ever by our sides.

But those of us who served in the First World conflict will remember how the experiences of those years of War were slowly – almost imperceptibly – smoothed away by the healing hand of time, until the grimmer memories were almost forgotten and only the less unpleasant ones remained.

So it will be with us.

It is in one sense true that nothing can restore the years which the locusts have eaten, but let us remember that these need not have been wasted years, they can have been redeemed, in part, if only we have made up our minds to go back into the world of free men as those who have seen a vision - a vision of what life may and can be in the future – of what we can make of life, and what life, by God's grace can make of us – and have prepared ourselves for that task.

We have learned many lessons in this place – the art of doing without so many things we considered vitally essential – the value of simple things – a greater self reliance – the ability to turn our hands to fresh endeavours – our minds to new pursuits.

For many this captivity has been a time of awakening to the reality of spiritual things – the worth of prayer and sacrament – a deeper faith and trust in God – a fuller knowledge of that glorious heritage of our Faith – the sword of the Spirit which is the word of God.

For some, there may be dark days still ahead – news of which they know nothing at the moment that may await them – news which may tend to shake their faith in God and man. Remember then, my Brothers, in the darkness of that hour that NOTHING, NOTHING, NOTHING can separate us from the love of God – if only we are prepared to acknowledge ourselves to be his children. The fact that we have survived to this hour is surely sufficient proof of that to us.

We have met here tonight to thank Him for that crowning mercy. If there is within us one shred of human gratitude, every day of our lives will be an endless thanksgiving.

But let us use this service for one purpose more – a solemn reconsecration of ourselves to the service of God and of our fellow men.

If we are honest with ourselves we must confess, each one, that we have done many things in this place which we ought not to have done, and left undone much that we ought to have done, but let us leave the memory of the faults and failings of others because we are only too conscious of the many faults and failings within ourselves.

Let us determine that we will be better men, better Christians, better husbands, better fathers, better sons and better citizens – pledged to devote all our skills and energy to the stupendous task that lies before us – the reconstruction of the life and prosperity of those countries to which we are each so proud to belong

A few minutes ago we paused in our hour of rejoicing, to give a thought to those thousands of our comrades whose bodies we leave behind in the soil of Malaya and the islands and seas of the Far East. We stood to attention while the Last Post and Reveille were sounded in their honour – our last united tribute to the memory of very brave and gallant men:

But we shall meet and greet in the closing rank
Of time's declining Sun,
When the bugles of God shall sound the call,
and the battle of life is done
There is no Death

One last word. I am told that the peasants of Spain use these words as they part from one another; 'Vaya con Usted'

I pass them on to you tonight, first of all in my Master's name, as His command, and then as His Benediction for your homeward journey, and your onward way across the years to be:

Go WITH God – GO with GOD.

Letters Section

Our first letter is from a man I am pleased and proud to call my friend although at the time of writing we have never met, but we have spoken to one another on the telephone many times now, and have written to one another a few times. He first heard me talking on BBC Radio Lancashire and below is the first letter Bill sent to me.

Letter from Mr Bill Lawrenson, Ashton-on-Ribble, Preston, Lancashire....

Dear Michael,

I thoroughly enjoyed our conversation on the 'phone today and I am now looking forward so much to receiving your book. Whilst I fought in the 14th Army throughout the Burma Campaign, I was fortunate enough not to be taken prisoner by the Japs.

On one occasion when we came into contact with some of the British and Australian prisoners of war, their horror stories were almost unbelievable, until we saw these things ourselves. One lad from the death railway gang told me that one day the Jap guards promised them they would be allowed to have their mail from home which the Japs had held back from them for nearly a year. You can imagine how much this would have meant to our boys to be able to hear at last from their loved ones. They were told if they could build another 10 metres of railway that day they could have their mail. They dragged their weary bodies and pulled out all they had left to try and do this in the hope of getting their letters. That seemed like a wonderful prize to them for their efforts.

They did manage the extra 10 metres although it took so much out of them and many fell by the wayside in the attempt. The Japs then made them parade in the full heat for hours before they brought out the sacks of mail and emptied them out in a heap on the floor in front of the men. With what little strength they had left in their bodies they gave a feeble cheer but their smiles were soon wiped out as the Jap guards just set fire to the heap of letters in front of them and stood and laughed and jeered at them. Those that did lose control and retaliated soon met their end, which of course is just what the guards wanted. No wonder our dear FEPOWS hated them so much.

They told me that food was so short that when they received their half a cup of rice a day it was crawling with maggots and cockroaches but they would just mash them in to the rice and eat them for they were so hungry. They told me if they could catch a frog then it was just pulled apart and eaten raw. I thought we had it bad but these poor souls had hell on earth, God alone knows how any of them survived.

I think the worst I ever saw was on one occasion we came to six poor lads hanging from trees. They had been very badly beaten and their genitals had been cut off and stuck in their mouths. One poor young chap who must have been the fattest of them had also been striped naked and bound as tight as he could be in barbed wire then the bits of his flesh that stuck out were cut off by the Japs swords and the poor chap left to bleed to death.

We learnt later that the Japs would get drunk on saki and then carry out these atrocities. I know of the tossing of (mostly Chinese) new born babies into the air and of how they would catch them on the ends of their bayonets. It made me sick then and still does to this day if I think too much about it. I saw once how they had raped all the nuns working at a hospital, as you say Michael "only God can forgive them" but like you I hope and pray that such things never happen again and that mankind can live in peace with one another and share our knowledge for a better tomorrow.

Michael, I am now blind and in my 80th year, so I hope you can read this alright as I now have to write by feel and memory. I wish you all the very best and lots of luck in your quest to tell the world the truth.

Yours sincerely,
Bill Lawrenson

Dear Bill,

Many thanks for your letters and 'phone calls and for sharing your experiences of those nightmare times. My father always said how much he owed to the boys of the 14th Army and of how every time a train load of Japs came by on the death railway on their way to Burma, he would smile and say "on you go, our boys will take care of you once you arrive. Enjoy your trip because its one way for you". We spoke of how they could not take the risk of leaving your dear comrades alive if they got wounded as it was impossible to take them along in such conditions, as your letter and many others I have received prove only too well.

Bill, I hope you were not offended when we spoke on the 'phone and you told me how you became blind. All I thought to say was how can you read my books then? You soon put me right and told me of how one of your comrades and friend makes sure you are OK and of how he will read the books to you. I should have known by now what comradeship means to you brave men. Bill, take care and God bless and keep you safe. From all of us we thank you for what you gave for our today and thanks for your part in freeing my dad and his fellow FEPOWS.

Your most sincerely, Michael

Letter from Jim Stoddart, Skegness, Lincolnshire.....

Dear Mike,

So nice to hear you on BBC Radio Lincolnshire. You spoke so movingly of those nightmare days that I just had to write and 'phone you to thank you for all you are doing. You know of all the suffering the Japs put our boys through, of which I was one. I ended up in Japan at a place called Oami in the factories. I was a medical man and was the one to care for our work parties. The Japs called me Abru Mitsu (the idle one). But I assure you I was not idle when they beat one of my comrades near to death. It was all I could do to keep them alive, and once a man was sick he was no good to them, so they picked on him even more. The first free European man I saw was a Commando who came into our camp to tell us we were now free men. The Americans had dropped us leaflets and supplies a few days earlier but what a sight it was to see this man – he was armed up to the hilt and if he had made contact with the Jap guards they would have known about it but they had all run off.

We were taken to Yokohama by train and the first two people I saw were two Salvation Army Officers, a man and wife –where they came from God only knows, but they gave us medical supplies and cared for us. I have never forgotten those two people and to this day I admire the good work that the Salvation Army does for others.

On the trip home we called at many wonderful places and one Australian chap who had been a prisoner at Changi at the Japanese surrender gave me a photo of one of the Jap Officers that had been executed on Changi beach. I think he was one that had been so hateful and cruel to our boys – they could not wait for any war trial for him. I have sent you the photo *[see photo section]* as I know it will be of interest to you. I thank you for all that you and your wife do for us poor old FEPOWS and say all power to your pen old son – you can't beat true stories and you have the gift of writing from the heart so keep it going. My wife and I wish you every success.

Yours thankfully,
Jim Stoddart

Letter from Angela Richardson, Lincoln.....

Dear Mr Bentinck,

I really enjoyed listening to you speaking to Melvyn Prior on BBC Radio Lincolnshire. You have such a gift of telling of those terrible times, and you do it in such a caring way that one can tell that you are speaking from the heart. I do hope it will not be too long before we, the people of Lincolnshire, can have you back on our radio, but until then please send me copies of your books. My reason for wanting to read them is that my dear uncle Norman, who died last year, was a prisoner of the Japanese. He would not talk about his days of suffering, even though he suffered for the rest of his life because of it. I think he did tell my dad a few stories towards the end of his life but I feel that I and my family should know of what men like your father and my uncle Norman gave for our today. I, like many others, think everyone should buy your books to support you in your efforts to help these brave men and also in the hope that it shows them what happened and prevents it from ever happening again, so please keep up your good work.

Yours sincerely,
Angela Richardson

Letter from Miss Jean Lewis, London.....

Dear Mr Bentinck,

I have just managed to buy your books "My Dad My Hero" and "Forgotten Heroes". I have already passed them on to numerous friends (please forgive me – I know they should really buy them) but I was so moved by them that I could not stop talking about them. I first heard you talking to Jerremy Dry on London News Talk – what a programme it was, so very moving. I think it was just before V.J. Day.

The next day I went to two W.H. Smith shops in London but they did not have any. The following Sunday I went away for a few days to Norfolk to Great Massingham only to read in the Mallard, their local magazine, that Robert Driver would be leading their V.J. Day parade, along with his wife Doris. I knew I had heard you mention a little of Robert's story from your book "Forgotten Heroes" while talking to Jerremy Dry. I knew I had to keep trying to find your books and the very next day I found them at W.H. Smiths book shop in King's Lynn. I have now read all the stories which I must say are so sincerely written. Thank you so much for putting your gift to such a good cause.

I was lucky enough to have a seat at the V.J. Day celebrations at Buckingham Palace, and will always treasure the poppy that I caught from the Lancaster bomber that flew over – such a wonderful occasion to see those brave men honoured at last for I don't need to tell you how much we owe them.

I was only 17 on V.J. Day those 50 years ago, so I can remember the war very well. I now look forward to reading your next book.

Yours sincerely,

Jean M. Lewis

Letter from Mrs Connie Baker, Camberley, Surrey.....

Dear Mr Bentinck,

I have recently returned from a pilgrimage to Singapore which was arranged by the Royal British Legion in order to pay my last respects to my young brother who was killed in the last battle to save Singapore on the 15th February 1942. He was always one of the unknown soldiers.

As I say, he was in those last battles around Adams Park and Bukit Tima, Singapore. It is only in the last four months that my eldest brother and I found out about the Kranji war graves memorial with his name on as we never even knew it existed. You can imagine how we felt. After 50 years this has come as quite a shock to us, as well as a surprise. However, my main reason for writing to you is that I met so many dear old FEPOWS on this trip that I learnt more about that war than I ever knew before. All of the FEPOWS told me to read Michael Bentinck's books about our war. They said "then you will know what your brother went through".

I got your books from W.H Smiths as soon as I got home and sat and read them through. You have written them so very well that I felt I was there with them. I cried, I laughed, but I could not put them down until finished. I was interested to see that in "Forgotten Heroes" that Bill Moody's story tells how he was in the Cambridgeshire's – the same regiment as my dear brother. I was wondering if Bill was still alive. Would you be kind enough to put me in touch with him as I have spoken to many people now about my brother, but none of them can tell me how he died. I wonder if Billy can help me. I would be so grateful to you, as I am for all the things I have learnt from reading your books. My brother was:

Corporal Ronald Frederick Stubberfield
6021034, D Company. 1st Btn
Royal Cambridgeshire Regiment
Much of his training was done at Norfolk and he was in the regimental police before going to the Far East. The last letter my parents had from him was from Bombay, India on 12th January 1942.
Yours sincerely,
Connie Baker

Dear Connie,

You will have received my letter by now with all the help I can give you with reference to your dear late brother, but if anyone can help us more after reading your letter to me, I will put them in touch with you.

Letter from Mr A.G. Hurtley, Suffolk.....

Dear Mr Bentinck,

I have just finished reading "My Dad My Hero" and "Forgotten Heroes". What can I say – so moving and so true, for you see I also was a prisoner of the Japanese for three and a half years. I feel I knew your father at that time for I was also in many of the camps that he was in. I can relate to so much of the pain he suffered, as we all did. He would have been so proud of you, as we all are. I can't wait to read your next book so keep up the good work for you have a God-given gift my son. How right you were in calling us Forgotten Heroes but thanks to you we now feel at last people will know the truth.
Yours most sincerely,
Mr A Hurtley

Letter from Jean Newman, London......

Dear Mr Bentinck,

Please find enclosed cheque to cover cost of your book "Forgotten Heroes" with autograph if you have not got writers cramp yet please. I would just like to say how interesting it has been listening to you on London News Talk with Jerremy Dry speaking about your dear late father and his comrades' stories. Thank God they shared them with you before it was too late. I can see now why so many men can't bring themselves to talk about it but I feel sure those men that have opened their hearts and minds to you must feel a relief come over them and they must be so pleased to know that the son of one of them is doing so much to help them. Like you I cannot imagine how human beings can do such things to fellow humans and I pray that it never happens again.

I wish you all my very best wishes for you deserve success. Everyone should read your books, for I know it would help such things from ever happening again.

Best wishes,

Jean Newman

Letter from Norman Bradley, Manchester......

Dear Michael,

I have just finished reading your books, which I thank you for as I received them by return of post so quickly. I have heard you twice now on BBC Radio GMR. You certainly have a great radio voice and your subject is so very moving that I could listen to you all day. I think you should make some tapes for us to buy.

Anyway I read your first book on a train journey and I became so engrossed in it that I missed my stop and had to catch a train back once it stopped again. I hope that shows you the power of your story. I found your other book just as good and things from it stuck in my mind for ages, I think the main one was just how lucky my generation have been in not having to suffer like your dad.

I feel that after this special 50th Anniversary with all the TV coverage that surely our government must know how we the people of the country hold these men in such high esteem, so why won't they see to it that those of them left alive receive at once the compensation they so richly deserve. Please send copies of your books to John Major, if he has a heart he cannot fail but see to it that compensation is given to them at once.

Yours thankfully,
Norman Bradley

Dear Norman,

I have received so many letters such as yours that I have taken your advice and sent Mr Major the books. I have received the following reply.

10 DOWNING STREET
LONDON SW1A 2AA

From the Correspondence Secretary

6 June 1995

Dear Sir,

I am writing on behalf of the Prime Minister to acknowledge your recent letter which is receiving attention.

Yours faithfully,

MRS FRANCES SLEE

Mr M Bentinck
10 Henry Morris Road
IMPINGTON
CB4 4YG

Letter from Mrs L Bennett, London.....

Dear Mr and Mrs Bentinck,

I am so pleased to offer my support in ordering your books and whilst writing I would just like to say how much I thank you both for all your hard work with the FEPOWS. I have always believed that the suffering and pain endured during those dreadful times must have been so traumatic that no wonder these dear men could not speak about it. My own father was like this but then we heard you on the radio and we both cried, but thanks to you he started to talk about it all and it has brought us even closer, so thank you so much for your written word – it has shown me so much of what my dear father went through for my today.

I know, like you, that we can never repay them, but thanks to people like you and your wife we are now beginning to have some understanding – even if it is 50 years later. I believe very strongly that our heroes must never be forgotten again. Thank you so much for your work.

Yours sincerely,
Linda Bennett

Letter from Mrs Joan Baker, Gt Yarmouth, Norfolk.....

Dear Mr Bentinck,

Many thanks for sending the books so quickly, it's always so nice to hear you on our Radio Norfolk. Your books have taught me so much about our dear FEPOWS, for you see I had two dear brothers who fought and suffered in that horrific campaign. Thankfully one is still alive but the other died in the fighting against the Japanese so at least he was spared the three and a half years of suffering but I still miss him so much after all these years. I now know what he gave for his country. My other brother and I do admire you and your wife so much for the wonderful work you are doing, so I am making my cheque for that little bit more to help the funds.

My very best wishes to you both.
Yours very sincerely,
Joan Baker

Letter from Mrs J Hall, Leicester.....

Dear Mr and Mrs Bentinck,

I have been meaning to write to you for some time now but alas I never seem to put pen to paper. I have enjoyed reading your books in a sad sort of way. The tears – I have shed them just uncontrollably and so has my daughter. We both agree we would not have missed them, you must try and find a big publisher to take these wonderful books on because they deserve to be sold world-wide. If you do write any more please put me top of your mailing list. What really made me write is that I have a picture of the liner Ormonde hanging on my wall, for my Aunt Rose Ashdown was a first class stewardess on the liner but retired just as the war began. She worked for P & O lines all her working life and lived on Canvey Island when on leave.

I send you both my very best wishes and thanks for all your help. Please keep up your wonderful work.

Yours sincerely,

Mrs J Hall

As many of you will know, SS Ormonde was used as a hospital ship to bring so many of our dear FEPOWS home and like Mrs Hall I am sure it holds many happy memories for so many of them for it brought them back to their dear old England to fulfil their dreams.

Letter from Mr R Wilkinson, Lancashire.....

Dear Mr Bentinck,

I must first of all say how much I enjoyed listening to you on BBC Radio Lancashire. I always love true stories and to hear you talking with so much feeling for these brave men really moved me. I was so moved I did not manage to get down your address but our Radio Lancashire are very helpful and they have passed it on to me. I would like a copy of "My Dad My Hero" please – as you said, what else could you have called it. I must say that over the years I have felt great sadness for the way in which former prisoners of war have been treated and neglected, especially those that suffered at the hands of the Japanese. I suppose it's not much use going on about it but I am old enough to have experienced a little of war time service in Holland and Germany before the war in Europe finished. I still get quite emotional at the thought of it. But at least we never suffered like those brave FEPOWS. If only our government felt as you do about their care. Keep up your good work and please let me know if you write another book and please do come back on to our radios soon.

With all my thanks.

Yours sincerely,

R Wilkinson

Letter from Alan Jones, Cardiff.....

Dear Michael,

I write to thank you for all your help to me and my family in tracing friends of my late father. As you know I never knew my father, as on that day when he set sail for the Far East, he did not know that mother was expecting me. My mother never remarried as she always said he was the only man for her. Now that I am older I admire her so much for that, for looking back I can see it was not easy for her bringing us up, my sister and I that is, without a dad, but we did not want for anything. She gave us enough love to make up for dad but it would have been so nice to have known my dad. We always thought he had died in the fighting but thanks to you we now know he died as a prisoner on the death railway.

Michael, as I read your books I could see just what he went through and suffered for us all but I still wish I had known him for the two chaps that you put me in touch with who were with him right up to his death spoke so wonderfully of him that I now know he really was a special man and although I never knew him, I am just so proud that he was my dad.

Yours thankfully,

Alan Jones

Dear Alan,

I am so pleased that I could be of help to you. As I have said many times, I was so lucky to have a wonderful father and even luckier to have known him and his love. I know how proud you are of your dad, as we all are, and Alan, he would have been so proud of you too. I am sure that in that far better place that all FEPOWS go to, he watches over you as my father does me, for as I write I know he is there helping me and I know that you have said to me that you feel this too, so you just live your life for you and your father for I know that with all that love in your heart just how good a person you are. Always be proud to say that you are the son of a brave FEPOW.

God bless you.

Letter from Mrs J Tookey, Kent.....

Dear Mr Bentinck,

I was fascinated, horrified and very very moved by all that you said on radio yesterday. Counselling is such a widespread thing nowadays that it is in danger of becoming a bit of a joke. I myself am a Victim Support Counsellor but oh, if only those poor brave souls who were Far Eastern Prisoners of War had had the help they so desperately needed once they were released....

Talking finally to you must have been of enormous help to your father, but I know it must have put a great strain on you while writing his life story. I feel though that it will be of so much help to so many others that have bottled it all up for so long.

Please send me copies of your books and let me know when any others that you write are ready as I think you said you would be publishing the memories of other brave men. I was in Singapore many years ago and I took flowers to Kranji war cemetery then went on to Changi prison. I was horrified to find that there was no memorial at all at this time for all those that had suffered and died there. I spoke to one of the guards at the gate then I just walked in and laid my flowers on the grass and said my silent prayer. I think the poor guard was so amazed that he did not think to stop me but I had made my point for without the sacrifice of men like your father, people like me would never have travelled as we do today. So God bless them all, I think that today this has been put right and now a memorial is in pride of place.

With all my very best wishes.

Yours sincerely,

Jill Tookey

Letter from Mr Alan Whitehill, Liverpool.....

Dear Michael Bentinck,

I read with great interest the article in the Guardian newspaper on August 14th which gave details of the two books you have written about your father and his comrades' war experiences in the Far East in the second world war. This is a topic so very close to my heart as my own father was also a Japanese prisoner of war.

I don't know whether it is coincidence or because of the publicity surrounding the 50th Anniversary of V.J. Day, but my father has begun ever so slightly to talk about those events in his life all those years ago. From his comments and from other sources, I'm trying to give myself an understanding, if that's actually possible, of what life was like during that period. I have heard so many people mention your books and of how true they are to what really happened, that I'd be grateful therefore if you could send me copies of the two books mentioned by John Ezard of the Guardian.

I also know that through your research you will have come into contact with other very interesting material. If possible I would appreciate any recommendations as to anything you think may help me to learn more of those times.

I look forward to hearing from you in the near future.

Yours sincerely,

Alan Whitehill

Letter from Mrs J Heywood, Doncaster, South Yorkshire.....

Dear Sir,

I wondered if you would be so kind as to send me copies of your books. I listened with interest and sorrow to an interview you gave on BBC Radio Humberside on Friday 10th November, the day before Remembrance Day, to Judi Merton. In fact I was in tears all the while I was preparing lunch while listening. I'm sure my father-in-law would be so interested in your books, and of course I would love to read them. I don't think anything I have ever heard or seen on television has ever moved me so much – it was the sadness and the sincerity in your voice that came through so very well.

I do hope the world will also be moved by your words and that we can now all live in peace for ever more.

I hope I have enclosed the right amount. Please do let me know if not.

My kindest regards to you.

Yours sincerely,

Mrs J Heywood

Letter from John Blake, Humberside.....

Dear Michael,

I hope you won't mind me using your first name but after listening to your programme on Radio Humberside with Judi Merton, I felt a bond with you, for I am the son of a dear FEPOW. My father has never spoken of those times in his life to me but we sat and listened to you together. I cried and he cried and after you finished we looked at one another and he said to me "I know you want me to tell you about my times with the Japs don't you?". "Please, if you feel you can," I replied. Well Michael we sat talking for the rest of that day, talking and crying together, just like you and your dear late father had done. He told me how he had seen one of his friends crucified to a tree by the Japs plus so many more horrific stories that I never even knew about. It has brought us so close – even though he always has been my hero, I feel he is now even more special to me. However could they do those things to our fathers? May God forgive them, for I can't. My father now tells me he feels so much better for sharing it all with me and Michael it is all thanks to you, for if we had not heard you on our radio he would never have opened his heart to me and I would never have known about it all.

Please send me your books which dad and I shall read together as his eyesight is not too good these days.

Keep up the good work you are doing.

Yours gratefully,

John Blake

Letter from D. Fullylove, Pemtre, Mid Glamorgan, Wales.....

Dear Mr Bentinck,

I look forward to reading your new book so much. Sorry I get so emotional when I speak to you on the 'phone about my dad, even though I never knew him personally as I was born in April 1939 and dad was killed February 4th 1942, aged 30. He was serving with 241 Battery, Royal Artillery. As I said on the 'phone, he is buried in a war grave in Jararta cemetery, Indonesia.

Thanks for all your help. I'll write again after reading your books.

Yours sincerely,

D Fullylove

Letter from Mrs J Henderson, Bristol.....

Dear Sir,

After hearing the wonderful programme that you gave on BBC Radio Bristol with Paul Bartrop about the poor prisoners of war, I would like a copy of your book please. What a courageous man your dear father was, and I also admire the son too. Your father would have been so proud of the work you are doing to help his comrades so keep it up and good luck to you.

Yours faithfully,
J Henderson

Letter from Mrs E Rushton, Salisbury, Wiltshire.....

Dear Mr Bentinck,

My son has sent me newspaper articles about a book you have written "My Dad My Hero", as my husband was five and a half years in that part of the war and because of it suffered for the rest of his life. He died nine years ago through a related illness to those horrific times for him. I am now a housebound widow of 83 and a real sufferer of vicious arthritis. My only comfort now is reading and I would be so pleased to read your book as I think we should remember those brave men now and for ever more.

Yours sincerely,
Ellen Rushton

Letter from Mr Roy Firth, Hull, North Humberside.....

Dear Sir,

Would you please forward me a copy of "Forgotten Heroes" as I was lucky enough to hear that special programme that you did with Judi Merton on BBC Humberside. I was a member of the RAF stationed in Singapore and Malaya from May 1948 until December 1950. I witnessed the places our dear boys were kept as prisoners. It was bad enough for us living there in 1948 without being prisoners and although we were deprived of little luxuries, my sympathies lie with your father and the rest of those brave boys for as the saying goes, seeing is believing. Previous to us arriving in Tengah, Singapore, there had been a near mutiny at Changi, the reason being that troop ships were being used to return the Japs to their homeland, leaving a lot of our lads out there well over their time for demob. This plan was soon changed and order restored. We also had a squadron of Australians on the camp who were very bitter about our Officers surrendering Singapore. I really do believe that they and our boys all wanted to fight on.

You are doing a good job old son, keep it up.

Yours faithfully,

Roy Firth

Letter from Carol Lynn Smith, Hertfordshire.....

Dear Michael,

I would love to purchase your books and I hope you won't mind me telling you a bit about my father who was a Chindt in Burma, so I have such an interest in your books. My father knew only too well the viciousness of the Japs as they dare not even leave their own wounded alive for the Japs to find. Imagine having to put your best mates to death if they got badly wounded rather than leave them to the Japs.

I have read and collected many books about the Chindt Campaign like General Wingate. I also often go to military fairs on the lookout for memorabilia. I have my father's medals and as you will know they are so very precious to me, as sadly my dear father died three years ago. But, like your father, he was a hero and we must never let people forget what they gave for our generation.

Many people think of doing something to help but my thanks to you, Michael, for you are doing something positive – keep it up and good luck.

Yours sincerely,

Carol Lynn Smith

Letter from Daphne Mason, Southampton, Hants.....

Dear Michael and Hilary,

I would love to purchase a copy of your book "Forgotten Heroes". I found your first book so moving – a harrowing insight into what so many of our dear men had to endure at the hands of the Japanese. Although I was only nine years old when V.J. Day arrived, I can remember it quite vividly – at last the war was really over and my dad would be coming home. My dad was in the Merchant Navy and was on various convoys to Russia and America, the Pacific etc. He was torpedoed but fortunately survived and was picked up at sea a few days later but by then many of his mates had slipped away. He rarely spoke of his experiences but one thing that stuck in his mind was his visit to Hiroshima, not long after the dropping of the bomb. The thing that remained in his mind was, however, the horrific photographs shown of the atrocities to our men and all the allies and particularly the English and Australian nurses, many of them shown left on galvanised roofs to bake to death after being raped etc. He never forgave them for this and if the Japanese were mentioned he would use the same expletives, "the little yellow b----". He would never buy Japanese products and God forgive us if we did.

Michael, my interest in reading books such as yours is like those recently held hostage today and all those years ago – it is the stamina of these prisoners, for in all these harrowing experiences it would appear it is not always those that are physically fit who necessarily survive but in the main those who are mentally strong and it is my interest and admiration that leads me to read books such as yours.

Wishing you every success in the sale of your books.

Best wishes to you both.

Daphne Mason

Dear Daphne,

Thank you for your wonderful letter. I feel that men like your father always seem to get forgotten. You know only too well how much we owe to the men of the Merchant Navy during the war and if I write a fourth book I plan to cover a true story of one of these brave men.

Yours thankfully,

Michael

Letter from Mrs I Faulkner, Southsea, Hants.....

Dear Mr Bentinck,

Please find cheque enclosed for £21 to cover two copies of "Forgotten Heroes" since I first heard you on our local BBC Radio Solent. I have heard so much about your books and of the good work that you and your wife do for our FEPOWS. Your first book was read many times by myself and my family and was sent out to Canada where it has been read by many and has now travelled thousands of miles which of course "Forgotten Heroes" will do also for we aim to help you to keep the FEPOWS memory alive for the next generation to know about why they have a life today.

Keep up the good work.

Yours sincerely,

I Faulkner

Letter from Mrs Jean Shaw, Lancashire.....

Dear Mr Bentinck,

Please send me a copy of "My Dad My Hero" for which I enclose a cheque for £10. Your radio programme with Bob Roberts was so very moving. I am sure the Far Eastern Prisoners of War must feel so very proud of the good work you are doing for them. I was an ATS driver during the war and was on the docks at Liverpool when the first ship load of FEPOWS arrived from Japan and the Far East. I and those with me were just struck dumb – yes, the shock was so great for here were young men just like skeletons. Their poor drawn faces told all and this was months after their release, it will be a sight I will never forget.

Thank you for all that you and your dear wife are doing for them.

Yours sincerely,

Jean Shaw

Letter from Mrs J B Irons, Colchester, Essex.....

Dear Mr Bentinck,

It was so good of you to chat to me on the 'phone last night about your books and of the work you do to help the brave FEPOWS. As I said, I first heard you on BBC Radio Essex but like a fool I mislaid the address and details. I enclose my cheque to cover cost as I know this will be something that my husband and I and my family will want to read.

I was six years old when the war was declared and spent the entire war with my parents in North London (together with the blitz, doodle bugs and buzz bombs). My five brothers were all on active service in the army so obviously from a young age I was very aware of what was happening. We all listened to every news bulletin and list of casualties on the wireless and we visited the cinema twice weekly to see the Pathe News. I can still picture my poor mother's face when the telegram arrived with news that my youngest brother had been killed in action – what can one say? You just have to hope and pray that it was quick for him and tell yourself that he was spared from being a prisoner but it always hurts for his young life was just wasted. Another of my brothers was one of the Forgotten Army in Burma but he survived and we've always been thankful that he was not captured or wounded by the Japanese. The other three came through relatively unscathed so knowing how badly other families suffered, I realise we came through the war reasonably well, but the strain on my parents with all their boys at war must have been pretty bad. I am sorry to ramble on and I do really hope that your books are best sellers. With all my best wishes.

Yours most sincerely,
Joan Irons

Letter from Kenneth Smallbridge, Devon.....

Dear Michael,

I was lucky enough to hear you speaking to Douglas Mounce on our local BBC Radio – so very moving, for you see I too was a Far Eastern Prisoner of War. I must have met your brave father at sometime during those nightmare days at the hands of the Japs for I too was in all of the camps that you mentioned, and I can remember many a poor chap being beaten to death – it's just something we all have to live with every day. Your book "My Dad My Hero" was so true to life at that time, so please forward on to me your book "Forgotten Heroes" which I'm sure will be just as good, so cheerio for now Michael – I'm still taking the tablets!

Yours thankfully,
Ken Smallbridge

Letter from Mrs Diana Sparkes, Southampton.....

Dear Mr and Mrs Bentinck,

Please forward copy of new book which I am most pleased to order. I 'm sure you will be interested to know that I shall be visiting Changi in November en route to the UK from Australia. I personally have been once before but it will be my husband's first visit. We wish to be there to take part in the 50th Anniversary of V.J. Day to honour the memory of my Aunt Josephine Foss who was imprisoned by the Japanese for three and a half years but she lived through all that they made her do and suffer and, yes, lived to be 96. But she, like all those in that horrific war, should never be forgotten.

Yours sincerely,
Diana Sparkes

Letter from Roy Curtis, Eastbourne.....

Dear Friend,

Please forward me details of your books for I heard you speaking on Southern Counties BBC – it was so moving I knew I had to find out more. One personal encounter I have seen of the Japs' action was in 1955. I met a man crawling along and he explained to me when I asked if I could be of help to him. He replied 'I'm like this thanks to the Japs, as I was a prisoner of theirs in the war and was tortured by them. They cut through my Achilles heel tendons and leg muscles – that's why I can't walk very well, but at least they spared my life so I am one of the lucky ones". I was so moved by him that it has stayed with me ever since. I hope to read your books to know even more than I already do of what these brave men gave for our today.

My very best wishes.
Roy Curtis

Letter from Mrs I Ireson, Worcestershire.....

Dear Mr Bentinck,

Having heard you once again with Gill Manley on our BBC Hereford and Worcester, I would like to have copies of your dear late father's stories as I am going to give them to my husband for Christmas. He, too, served in Burma and the Far East from February 1943 until June 1946 so I know he will want to read them, even though it will bring it all back to him. Thank you for what you are doing for our heroes. Looking forward to hearing you again with Gill soon, take care.

Yours sincerely,

R Ireson, Mrs

Letter from Mrs S Baker, Worcester.....

Dear Mr Bentinck,

Once again I have just heard you on BBC Radio Hereford and Worcester with Gill Manley – I sat absolutely riveted. I listened with a mixture of horror and such fascination to your first broadcast and found today just as moving and on the strength of this I must read the books. Please be kind enough to sign them for me and I hope we are lucky enough to hear you again next year.

Till then I send all best wishes.

Yours sincerely,

Mrs S Baker

Letter from T. Hutchison, Hereford.....

Dear Mike,

I was privileged to listen to today's programme on BBC Hereford and Worcester that you took part in with Gill Manley. I was a regular soldier and served from 1935 until 1945 for most of the war. I was in the Middle East and we had heard of some of the atrocities, but when 1 was posted to Singapore, I don't think even I could believe the atrocities that took place. When I heard of your books and the wonderful work that you and your wife are doing to help these brave men, I knew I had to read your books and contribute as well. My wife was with me in married quarters at Changi barracks and to this day she swears that those quarters were haunted by the horrific things that the Japanese had done to our allied prisoners there. Please keep up your good work and thank Gill Manley for having such interesting people as you on.

Yours sincerely,
T Hutchison

Letter from Mrs Elaine Benton, Hallow, Worcester.....

Dear Mr Bentinck,

I have just listened to you on Gill Manley's programme on Hereford and Worcester Radio – absolutely brilliant, so moving, I could have listened all day. I am far too young to remember the war years but thanks to people like yourself, we younger ones can learn of the truth from those terrible times and perhaps one day your wise words will come true to fruition. Please forward me both books, cheque enclosed, and once again thank you so much for the best radio programme I have ever heard.

Yours sincerely,
Mrs Elaine Benton

Letter from Mr Joe Williams, Evesham, Worcester.....

Dear Mr Bentinck,

I have listened to and been so very moved by your long chat with Gill Manley on Radio Hereford and Worcester this afternoon. As I was just a school boy during the war and even though I was spared most of the horrors of war, and the things that resulted from it, I shall never forget the Far East Prisoners of War and all that they were forced to endure, as you said. I shall certainly wear my poppy with pride for as you say we owe these men so much for our lives today. Please send me copies of both books and I wish you every success with the sales of your books and the good work you are doing.

Yours sincerely,
Joe Williams

Letter from Mr J Thomas, Bolton, Lancashire.....

Dear Michael Bentinck,

May I say how fortunate I was to have been in Worcester and just by chance heard you on BBC Hereford and Worcester. I was glued to the radio throughout – it was the type of programme that wins awards but I'm sure the BBC will know that. I would like copies of your books for my own dear father who served in the Far East during the war. Could you advise me if there are any recordings of your interviews available for purchase as I think it such a shame my own father did not hear how wonderful and sincere you spoke of your dear father and all the other brave men. If you have any recordings for sale, please let me know.

Yours sincerely,

J. Thomas

Letter from Mr Jack Roberts, Liverpool.....

Dear Mr Bentinck,

I listened to the wonderful programme that Linda McDermott of BBC Radio Merseyside broadcast on V.J. Day, all based on extracts from your book "Forgotten Heroes". It was so very moving and the actors that read the extracts from your book did it so very well. I think it fair to say it was the best radio programme I have ever heard on the subject of war and all so very true. It was nice to hear you speak of how you feel so privileged that the FEPOWS trust you with their stories but after reading your first book "My Dad My Hero", I must say that you have a gift old son, for it was just as if you had been there with us – it took me back to those nightmare days I can tell you.

Michael, I found the part where your father saw one of the chaps pushed off the Wampo viaduct so very moving for I lost my own brother like this. A Jap just punched him in the face so hard that it knocked him out and he fell to his death. I retaliated but the Jap hit me with his rifle in the stomach but luckily for me I managed to cling on to a teak railway sleeper as I fell. He put the boot in of course but I just clung on for dear life and having already killed my brother I did not care if he killed me as well but he did spare me, although I was punished again on our return to camp. My brother was buried in the camp cemetery so I imagine his remains are still there to this day. I am now 86 years old but I will never forgive them for what they did to us, for it was just bloody murder. To this day I miss my young brother for he was only 21 years old and had his whole life in front of him. You say we have marked the paths of history but my God I wish we had not for so many good people died such horrific deaths at the hands of our hateful captors.

I thank you for what you, as the son of one of us old soldiers are doing to help us, I hope you don't mind me writing to you as Radio Merseyside were good enough to give me your address after my friend got the book for me from W.H. Smiths in Liverpool. I hope you can make out my shaky writing but I blame my old age.

Yours sincerely,

Jack Roberts - Still a proud old FEPOW

Dear Jack,

What can I say to you? Nothing much to ease the pain of losing your dear brother in such a terrible way. All I know is that you are not alone for so many people tell me very similar stories. The saying "I was one of the lucky ones" comes to mind, for at 86 years old I'm sure you know how lucky you are. I hope you go on to enjoy being lucky for many many years to come and hope you receive your royal telegram from our Queen or King whichever is on the throne when you make your century.

Thanks Jack for our today. God bless you mate.

Michael

Letter from Mrs Muriel Challis, Cambridge.....

Dear Mr Bentinck,

I had the pleasure of meeting you and your wife, just before Christmas, when I called at your home, with my daughter, Linda. On that occasion I bought both of your books, "My Dad, My Hero" and "Forgotten Heroes".

I am writing now because, having read, and cried, then re-read my way through both books, I wanted to congratulate you on writing two of the most moving, and beautifully written, books I have ever had the pleasure of reading.

You may remember that I was friendly with Jim and Dulcie before, and during, the war years. Although we didn't see a lot of each other in recent years, I still remember them both with affection.

You already know that your Father was a very nice, and popular, man. I can understand why you felt such a strong desire to produce such a fitting tribute to his courage, and forbearance, in the face of such fear and suffering.

I am sure that he would have been so proud of your abilities as an author, and that he would have been deeply touched at all the care, thought, and effort you have put into your work in his memory.

There must be many ex-servicemen, who having read your books, have re-lived many memories, and, like me, cried many tears. These people have so many memories, most of which are ignored, or ridiculed, these days. We hope that such a war never happens again, but we should remember all those, such as your Dad, who are such great examples to us all. You, too, have much to be proud of, for the way you have remembered and recorded the events, from your father's memories.

It was a great pleasure to meet, and to be given such a warm welcome by, you and your wife. I will watch out, with interest, for further news on your progress as an author, and I hope that we will meet again one day.

Please give my best wishes to your Mum. I hope that she is keeping well. I am sure that she, too, is very proud of you, for your wonderful tribute to your Dad.

Congratulations, again, on your moving, and beautiful, masterpieces.

With best wishes,
Mrs Muriel Challis

Letter from Mr J Robinson, Birmingham.....

Dear Mike Bentinck,

I heard your interview on BBC Radio W.M. today and was so very moved for although it brought it all back to me, I am just so pleased to have heard you speaking so sincerely of your dear late father. I was in most of the camps you mentioned and I feel sure I can remember your father, the man who drove the Jap Executioner. I think his name was Jim and he was only about 20 years old but he was very good to the lads in the sick hut by smuggling in food for them. It's strange, but much of this food the Executioner knew about, and Jim would say how he just turned a blind eye to it – but that was the Japs for you Mike, one minute kind to you, the next they would strike out at you and beat you to death.

I lost my best friend like this when one of the guards just picked on him for no reason. He beat him so badly that he kicked his left eye right out of his head. It took my friend three days to die of his injuries, a thing I shall never forget. We had just been moved up to Thailand and had all been promised better camps and this is what we found. My friend was spared any more suffering and I made a promise to get even with the guard that murdered him but I was soon moved up country and missed my chance, but as you know it was all I could do to keep alive now without looking for trouble so this guard got away with it. I often wonder how many more of our boys he murdered. I just hope that if he survived the war and went home to Japan that he has had a terrible life and suffered in his mind every day because of what he did. I'm sorry to go on so, Mike, but thanks for what you and your wife are doing for us old boys. I can tell that you are a chip off the old block and your dear dad would be so proud of you. God bless you son.

Yours gratefully,
Jack Robinson, Birmingham

Letter from Mrs Doreen Dennison, Lancaster.....

Dear Michael,

Many many thanks for all your help to our dear FEPOWS. Please can you send me another copy of "My Dad My Hero" as I want to send it to friends abroad. You'll remember me, I'm Randall Maskell's sister and you and Mr Few of the Cambridge Yasume Club have been so kind in visiting him in Fulbourn Hospital in Cambridgeshire for, as you know, he is all I have left now as family, and as I am now in my 80's I cannot get out and about as I could so thank you so much for your reports on Randall. I know he is not at all well and I don't think he will ever come out again but I know he is in good hands. Last time I saw him he really had deteriorated but at least he still remembered me. Unfortunately my husband suffered a heart attack so we had to come home quick.

So thanks so much for all you do to help me and all the other relations of dear FEPOWS.

Yours thankfully,
Doreen Dennison

P.S. The books are off to Australia.

Dear Readers,
   Randall is suffering from mental war trauma – like dementia, but in Randall's case he still thinks he is in a Japanese prisoner of war camp. When I visit him he bows to you thinking you to be a Jap guard. He lines all the other patients up and shouts out in Japanese numbering. As if he did not suffer enough in those three and a half years of hell at the hands of the Japanese. His mind now still holds him a prisoner of those nightmare times.
   When people ask me why I do all I can to help the FEPOWS they should come with me to see Randall and the many like him. My God they would see then why I have to help them all I can.
   Yours most sincerely
   The Author

Our Last Letter....

From Mrs Alice Fairhurst, Adlington, Lancashire.....

Dear Mr and Mrs Bentinck,
   After reading your books we passed them on to our son Roger for his 52nd birthday. We were all so very moved by your written words of those terrible times. Roger has written a poem and has dedicated it to all that suffered at the hands of the Japanese, he hopes to have it published in our local paper for the 50th Anniversary of V.J. Day. I know he would be honoured to know that you would use it in your next book as we notice that you use a poem on the inside covers of your books. So if you feel you could use it, please do as I enclose a copy for your attention.
   Yours sincerely,
   Mrs Alice Fairhurst

Dear Mrs Fairhurst,
   I am only too pleased to use Roger's poem as usual. See page 160 and thank you Roger for your tribute to our dear Burma star boys and our FEPOWS.
   God bless you.
   Michael

Letter from Michael Bentinck - Author.....

Dear Friends,

    Just to say a big thank you for all your letters since October 1994 when my first book was published. I have received over 5,000 letters from you my dear readers all with a story to tell of yourselves or a dear loved one. The letters I have included I just picked at random as a way of trying to be fair. So many of you have let me know how much you enjoyed reading the letters section in "Forgotten Heroes" that I have done the same again.

    To all the dear people that have heard me on radio or seen me on TV I thank you all for your kind words and your valued orders for the books. I would like also to thank all the radio presenters and their producers for all their help, to people like dear Gill Manley who's programme I seem to take over and turn into all our yesterdays. I say thank you so much my love.

    To my mate Jerremy Dry of London News Talk, I also owe a very big thank you to as I do to all the friends I have made through the radio and TV work that I was privileged to do through the 50th Anniversary year. Last but not least the couple that gave me my first chance in radio work, yes Producer Clare Harrison and Presenter Christopher South of Radio Cambridgeshire.

    Yours thankfully,
Michael Bentinck

Well, dear friends, once again we have come to the end of our journey through this book, you have met two more of my dear brave heroes in Stanley and Percy, along with some more of my dear late fathers story. Once again I hope it has been a moving but worthwhile experience for you all, I know only too well from your letters how much you think of our dear FEPOWS and I thank you for that. To all of you that ordered your book through our mail order department (my wife Hilary), I thank you for your support. Hilary sends her love and best wishes to you all and we assure you that you are all in our prayers especially those of you that wrote to us to let us know that your dear husbands, fathers or grandads had departed our planet earth during this 50th Anniversary year to join their comrades in that far better place that they go to for as I have said many times, I know our Lord has a special place at his right hand side in heaven for all our FEPOWS. But for those of us left we have our memories of these wonderful men who gave their youth for us all so that we could have freedom and love in our world. They have marked the paths of history and now we that are left must work even harder to make sure that it was the war to end all wars. You won't need me to tell you the state our world is in today but as my father said "only good can overcome evil" and although he could not forgive the Japanese guards, I know he did not want us to hold it against the Japanese of today. Many of them today don't even know of what the generation before them did to our boys, and I am lucky that where I live near to Cambridge, with its big Universities, that younger Japanese who come to college here find my books and read them. They then go back to Japan and ask questions about what they have read and so they find out the truth about those nightmare days. Many of them have written to me to apologise for what their forefathers did and of how horrified they were to learn of it. As you know my hope is that as they learn about it all, it will stop such things ever happening again.

So my friends it just remains for me to thank you all for buying my books, for you are the ones that make it possible for me to be able to help our dear FEPOWS and as you will have seen from our letters many of them are still suffering today from the things they suffered all those years ago.

Yours,

Michael Bentinck

Author's £1,000 gift to Far East POWs

A WRITER chronicling the suffering of soldiers taken prisoner by the Japanese during the war is to give £1,000 to help survivors in West Norfolk.

Mike Bentinck will present the money to the chairman of Lynn area branch of the Far Eastern Prisoners' of War Association, Mr Fred Backham, of South Wootton, on Radio Norfolk on June 6.

Mr Bentinck (47), of Impington, near Cambridge, is visiting Radio Norfolk's Lynn studio to talk about his second book, Forgotten Heroes.

It includes the stories of Burma campaign veterans Mr Robert Driver, of Great Massingham, and Mr Bert Grimes, of Roydon.

They were among 5,000 people who contacted him after the publication of his first book, My Dad, My Hero.

The book was dedicated to his father, Jim, who retired to Snettisham, but died in 1990 from heart problems caused by a disease he contracted while a prisoner of war.

Mr Bentinck said he had been so moved by their stories that he wanted to donate some of the profits from the book to FEPOW.

"I hope the money will help other men suffering from tropical worms in their blood and war trauma dementia and the widows of former prisoners," he said.

A Poem by Roger Fairhurst

His heartfelt tribute to the Forgotten Army and FEPOWS

In a beautiful land of lush green terra firma
fought the men of the 14th of Burma,
along with other men and mules too,
they slogged through the jungle and mud like glue.
Many miles away in brutal conditions,
some of their FEPOW comrades built a railway in the south,
dying like flies,
never to see home,
hundreds died – died in their youth.
For them no comfort, no fireside or cold beer,
but for them a terrible brutal beating - a sadistic leer,
for theirs was the horrible and sad mishap
to be taken as prisoners of the cruel Jap.
But just a few years later back home,
the Japanese saw an explosion of mushroom shape,
terrible fires, terrible deaths;
for thousands of them there was no escape.
Japan is a land – a land of the rising sun
but on that day they felt the fire of two suns rolled into one.
We must never forget we have rising sons,
Gone are these men, the sound of the guns.
Forget their courage and suffering not at all,
God bless you boys, the long, the short and the tall.

By Roger Fairhurst, Adlington, Lancashire

Kohima Prayer

*When you go home tell them of us and say
for your tomorrow we gave our today.*
